MW00460200

Whispers *of* Mary

What Twelve
Old Testament
Women Teach Us
About Mary

GAYLE SOMERS

ASCENSION
West Chester, Pennsylvania

Excerpts from the English translation of the *Catechism of the Catholic Church* for use in the United States of America © 1994 United States Catholic Conference, Inc.–Libreria Editrice Vaticana. Used with permission. English translation of the *Catechism of the Catholic Church: Modifications from the Editio Typica* © 1997 United States Conference of Catholic Bishops–Libreria Editrice Vaticana.

Unless otherwise noted, Scripture quotations are from the Revised Standard Version of the Bible–Second Catholic Edition (Ignatius Edition) © 2006 National Council of the Churches of Christ in the United States of America. Used by permission. All rights reserved.

Scripture texts marked "NAB" in this work are taken from the New American Bible, revised edition © 2010, 1991, 1986, 1970 Confraternity of Christian Doctrine, Washington, DC, and are used by permission of the copyright owner. All rights reserved. No part of the New American Bible may be reproduced in any form without permission in writing from the copyright owner.

Ascension
PO Box 1990
West Chester, PA 19380
1-800-376-0520
ascensionpress.com

Design by Ashley Dias

Illustrations: p. 2: Rembrandt, *The Prophetess Anna* (1631), commons.wikimedia.org. p. 196: Botticelli, *Madonna of the Book* (1483), commons.wikimedia.org.

Printed in the United States of America
24 25 26 27 28 5 4 3 2 1

ISBN 978-1-954882-39-3 (trade book)
ISBN 978-1-954882-40-9 (e-book)

To my daughters,
Geneva Matthews, who first conceived the idea for this book,
and Leah Stephens, whose love of Scripture encouraged me to write it,

and my husband,
Gary, always confident I could do it,

and my granddaughters,
Seraphina, Beatrix, Gemma, and Giovanna Matthews,
to inspire them to become women of faith, handmaids of the Lord.

———————————

TABLE *of* CONTENTS

Introduction

"Throughout the Old Covenant the mission of many
holy women *prepared* for that of Mary."
–*Catechism of the Catholic Church* 489

"Your words were found, and I ate them, and your words
became to me a joy and the delight of my heart"
–Jeremiah 15:16

As I sit down in my study to begin this book, I see before me a print of Rembrandt's magnificent painting of Anna, the Prophetess, which has graced the wall of my study for many years. Anna was the elderly widow in the Temple in Jerusalem *"at that very hour"* Mary and Joseph presented the infant Jesus there in obedience to Jewish law (see Luke 2:22–38). She heard Simeon, a devout man whom God had promised would see with his own eyes Israel's long-awaited Messiah before he died, blessing God while holding the child. Anna spent the years of her widowhood in the Temple *"worshiping with fasting and prayer night and day."* She heard Simeon's announcement that here, at last, was *"the Lord's Christ."* She also heard Simeon's word to Mary about what lay ahead for her and her Child: *"Behold, this child is set for the fall and rising of many in Israel, and for a sign that is spoken against (and a sword will pierce through your own soul also), that thoughts out of many hearts may be revealed."*

Although St. Luke's description of Anna is brief, Rembrandt's painting helps us picture her devout life and its fruit. In the

painting, a light shines down from above over Anna's shoulder and onto her clothing, brightening it with a shimmering sheen. The light's focus, however, is on the large book she is reading, the Scriptures. Anna is completely absorbed in her reading, with her hand lying on a page, tracing its words. Although the details of her face are only lightly sketched and are shaded by her head covering, the woman is fully alive in her contact with God's Word. She would have been well acquainted with its ancient stories of the men and women through whom salvation history unfolded. When she heard Simeon's announcement about Jesus and his mother in the Temple, a spark of recognition ignited her soul. She knew the presence in the Temple of this mother and son heralded the beginning of Israel's redemption. As a prophetess, Anna understood that here was the culmination of the *meaning* of the book she loved so well. She was not able to keep this Good News to herself. So Anna, whose long life had been silently hidden away in the Temple, became the Lord's first evangelist in Jerusalem: "*She gave thanks to God, and spoke of him* [the child] *to all who were looking for the redemption of Jerusalem.*"

Why do I love this painting so much? I have taught the Scriptures to Catholic adults ever since my family and I became Catholics in 1995. Because of its unfamiliarity to many, the Old Testament often became the focus of my teaching. Like Anna, I have pored over its pages with what has sometimes felt like ecstasy to me, savoring every word. Being a woman, I have always enjoyed reading the stories of the women who were part of God's unfolding plan for his creation. So, in the COVID year of 2021, when my daughter and I decided to do a home Bible study for women (the churches were mostly shut down to all meetings other than Mass), I prepared a study on the theme of "Praying with the Women of Scripture." We began, naturally, with women in the Old Testament, and then something remarkable happened to all of us.

We worked our way through the stories of women who lived in each age of salvation history—reading passages of Scripture in which they spoke, sang, prayed, and acted. We were thrilled to receive from them lessons of faith, humility, courage, wisdom, perseverance, family life, leadership, conversion, suffering, and much more. Beyond that, we began to understand why the Church teaches that "the mission of many holy women *prepared* for that of Mary" (CCC 489). Most of the women in our study, who ranged in age from grandmothers to mothers of young children and everyone in between, had scant knowledge of some of these saintly Old Testament women and even less familiarity with how each in her own way was like a small tile that would eventually become a glorious mosaic of the Mother of God. Those ladies drank in every word. They were discovering the feminine Marian typology of the Old Testament.

In its simplest definition, typology is "the study of persons, places, events, and institutions ... that foreshadow later and greater realities made known by God in history."[1] Typology is a fundamental characteristic of Catholic biblical interpretation. The *Catechism* tells us, "The Church, as early as apostolic times, and then constantly in her Tradition, has illuminated the unity of the divine plan in the two Testaments through typology, which discerns in God's works of the Old Covenant prefigurations of what he accomplished in the fullness of time in the person of his incarnate Son" (CCC 128). By writing the story of what lay ahead for the healing of creation in the flesh-and-blood lives of men and women who lived before that healing arrived, God confirmed his astonishing promise at the time of the Fall in Eden—flesh and blood caused the wound, but flesh and blood would heal it in the Incarnation. Finding these types and discovering how they come alive to us is one of the great blessings of reading the Old Testament.

As we engaged with these women in our study, listening to their voices, many questions began to stir in us. What did Mary know of these women's stories? What might their voices have given her to prepare her to fulfill her mission as the mother of the Messiah? In our study, we came to love these women; we took them into our hearts. During Mary's life, did she too have them in her heart, pondering their examples?

We got some helpful answers to these questions, first from Scripture itself, and then from Pope Benedict XVI in his apostolic exhortation *Verbum Domini*. In St. Paul's second letter to Timothy, who had a Jewish mother and grandmother, he wrote, *"From childhood you have been acquainted with the Sacred Writings which are able to instruct you for salvation through faith in Christ Jesus"* (2 Timothy 3:15). The covenant people of God loved the Scripture; Jewish parents taught it to their children from an early age. Mary certainly would have known these stories—hearing them over and over. Then, Pope Benedict XVI gives us additional helpful guidance on the question of Mary's relationship with Scripture:

> The *Magnificat* ... is entirely woven from threads of Holy Scripture ... Here we see how completely at home Mary is with the word of God, with ease she moves in and out of it ... Since Mary is completely imbued with the word of God, she is able to become the Mother of the Word Incarnate.[2]

Pondering Mary's familiarity with the Word of God fired up more questions for us: If these stories of Old Testament women contributed to Mary's formation, can they also contribute to ours? The rest of our study helped us explore answers to that question. When we got to its end, many thought I should write it all down in a book (I admit I was not immediately keen on this idea). They wanted to understand it better, to read and reread the stories of these wonderful women who prepared the way for the mission of Mary. They treasured the valuable help we all received from them; they were particularly eager for their daughters and granddaughters to know and treasure it, too. My own daughter relentlessly pressed this idea home to me.

So, here is the little book I never intended to write. What kind of book is it? Because it came to life through Bible study, it is built primarily on Scripture stories. It is not scholarly or anecdotal. It is a "listening" book; we want to hear what these Old Testament women can say to us. In my long life of teaching the Bible, I have discovered that the best way to help Catholic adults engage with the actual text of Scripture is to ask lots of questions that require us to think carefully and even imaginatively about the words in front of us. This way is far more effective than simply telling people what the verses mean. So, there are many rhetorical, open-ended questions here. Pondering questions about the text helps prevent us from rushing through it; we are much better listeners as a result. In this way, we can answer the call of Vatican II, when the council fathers exhorted the faithful to "gladly put themselves in touch with the sacred text itself"[3] Why is contact "with the sacred text itself" so important? Reading Scripture is unlike any other reading we do because it alone is supernatural, both human and divine. We see the truth of this represented every time we go to Mass and watch the Scripture incensed during the Liturgy of the Word. Jesus is present in his Word, just as he is present in the Eucharist, which is also incensed. Other sacred reading—the lives and writings of the saints, catechisms, theological and devotional books—inspire and guide us; they *inform* us. Scripture alone has the power to *transform* us. As the council teaches, "In the sacred books, the Father who is in heaven meets his children with great love and speaks with them; and the force and power in the Word of God is so great that it stands as the support and energy of the Church … the pure and everlasting source of spiritual life."[4] Scripture is meant to "enlighten the mind, strengthen the will, and set men's hearts on fire with the love of God."[5]

Additionally, the fathers of Vatican II called us to pray with the Scripture: "And let them remember that prayer should accompany the reading of Sacred Scripture, so that God and man may talk together; for we 'speak to Him when we pray; we hear Him when we read the divine saying.'"[6] Therefore, each chapter of the book also includes a time for personal reflection and response to its Scripture story.

As we listen and pray in company with these women of Scripture, we will follow *The Bible Timeline*® Learning System through the time periods of salvation history in which they lived. This system, developed by Catholic Bible scholar Jeff Cavins and underpinning *The Great Adventure*® Bible Study Program, divides the Bible into twelve time periods. These twelve periods trace the great story of how God created man and woman, who rebelled against him, and how he did not abandon us but promised a Savior and sent that Savior in the fullness of time to redeem us from sin. The chart that follows shows where the women we will get to know in this book fall within the twelve *Great Adventure Bible Timeline* periods, along with the color coding that represents what happened during each stage of the story of salvation:

PERIOD	NARRATIVE BOOKS OF THE BIBLE	COLOR	WOMEN OF SCRIPTURE
Early World	Genesis 1–11	Turquoise, the color of the earth viewed from space	Eve
Patriarchs	Genesis 12–50	Burgundy, representing God's blood covenant with Abraham	Sarah
Egypt and Exodus	Exodus	Red, the color of the Red Sea	Miriam
Desert Wanderings	Numbers	Tan, the color of the desert	
Conquest and Judges	Joshua; Judges; 1 Samuel 1–8	Green, the color of the hills of Canaan	Rahab; Deborah and Jael; Hannah
Royal Kingdom	1 Samuel 9–31; 2 Samuel; 1 Kings 1–11	Purple, the color of royalty	Bathsheba
Divided Kingdom	1 Kings 12–22; 2 Kings 1–16	Black, representing Israel's darkest period	The desperate widow
Exile	2 Kings 17–25	Baby Blue, symbolizing Judah "singing the blues" in Babylon	
Return	Ezra; Nehemiah	Yellow, symbolizing Judah's return home to brighter days	Esther; Judith
Maccabean Revolt	1 Maccabees	Orange, the color of the fire in the lamps in the purified Temple	The mother of martyrs
Messianic Fulfillment	Luke	Gold, representing the gifts of the Magi	The Blessed Virgin Mary
The Church	Acts	White, the color of the spotless Bride of Christ	

My prayer for this book is that it will deepen us in the faith, hope, and love we see in these Biblical women. As they surely spoke to both Anna and Mary in their lives with God, may they speak to us as we walk with him, too. May their stories leave on our lips the words of our Mother: *"My soul proclaims the greatness of the Lord"* (Luke 1:46, NAB).

Chapter One

Eve—In the Time of the Early World

> "I have gotten a man with the help of the LORD."
>
> —Genesis 4:1

Historical Context: Early World (Creation–2200 BC)

Of all the stories of women in the Old Testament, perhaps none is better known than that of Eve. When we think of her, can we do it without seeing a shadow? Without thinking, "If only she hadn't reached for that fruit"? She does break our hearts, and that hurts. Yet there is something else true about her that we ought not to miss. Eve, a woman, stands at the center of the drama that begins our story in the Garden of Eden, the garden of God's delights.

In the Garden

Surely Eve's role at the center of the story must mean something more than just her failure. At the very least, it should prompt this question: Why did the Serpent set his sights on her? Why didn't he make his pitch directly to Adam, who was surely standing right there with her?

There have been many answers offered to this question over the years. Some have suggested that the Serpent's snub of

Adam was simply another expression of his complete rejection of God's authority over creation, since it was God who put Adam in charge of the Garden. Others have said that because of the differences between male and female, the Serpent thought Eve would be more vulnerable to the lure of the beautiful fruit. There is, however, another possible answer.[7]

We know God made both male and female in his image and likeness (see Genesis 1:26). Therefore, we can think of the masculine and feminine as his icons. An icon is a visible painted image of a holy person (or a scene in which he or she appears) that, when we look upon it, puts us in mind of the one it represents. Therefore, if we are images or icons of God, who is pure spirit and does not have a body, there is something written into our visible bodies that puts us in mind of the One who created us. Beginning with our physical bodies, we see the masculine was designed to initiate, to implant, to generate. The feminine was designed to receive, to be implanted, to gestate, to birth and nurture life. Because men are generally larger and stronger than women, they are naturally inclined to protect that which is weaker. Because women bear and nurture children, they are naturally dependent for protection and help for large portions of their lives. Thus, in an iconic, rhythmic way, the masculine gives; the feminine receives.

This rhythm of giving and receiving was also to be the rhythm of the whole creation, designed by God always to rely on him for its existence and continuance, utterly dependent on him. Even the human soul lives by this rhythm. This iconography is indelible, it cannot be erased. It exists independently from the individual who bears it. It is simply there in us by virtue of our creation, regardless of whether we acknowledge it or live it.

Both masculine and feminine reflect two foundational truths about God and his relationship with the world he created. The masculine represents God, the Creator and protector, and the feminine represents all creation—a willingness to wait on God, to receive what only he can give. Inherent in this feminine posture, of course, is humility. There is a smallness to it, an acceptance of dependence. So, when Eve reached for the forbidden fruit, lured by the fallen angel, her sin was not only that she grasped the fruit, just as Adam sinned when he grasped it from Eve's hand. It was that she grasped it as *woman*, a deep violation of her vocation and her iconic *meaning* for all the rest of creation. Life's meaning (to be receptive of God's action), written into the feminine icon, was turned upside down with that grasp.

If this is the way it was at creation, the Serpent's lethal aim at Eve makes sense. So much was at stake in her response to his temptation. On the one hand, we do certainly regret her choice; on the other, we should not let that blind us to the great significance of woman's feminine iconography. Women bear in themselves, by the imprint of God's own hand, the iconic meaning of all creation. This might surprise us, that God would invest so much in woman. Well, here is the wonder of it all: "Against all human expectation God chooses those who were considered powerless and weak to show forth his faithfulness to his promises" (CCC 489). The feminine vocation is a lofty one.

The Fall and the Promise

The fall of Adam and Eve, though catastrophic, was not the final act of the drama played out in the Garden of Eden. No, the one that followed it overcame and surpassed its tragic consequences. God did not give up on his human icons. After he cursed the

Serpent, he made an outrageous promise; indeed, if we had been standing in the Garden as observers hearing it for the first time, we would have fallen over backwards, felled through sheer astonishment. To his enemy God said, *"I will put enmity between you and the woman, and between your seed and her seed; he shall bruise your head and you shall bruise his heel"* (Genesis 3:15). There would come on the horizon of human history another woman and man to stand at the center of an even greater drama. In the Garden, it was a woman and her husband. Someday, it would be a mother and her son who would take up this battle, this *enmity*, and finish it with victory. What a stunning, humiliating defeat for the Serpent! The very flesh and blood upon which he preyed in the Garden—as he expected to strike a devastating blow to God by killing off his beloved creatures—would one day be his conquerors. This is enough to make us wonder if that was the reason God allowed him into the Garden in the first place.

From the moment God promised a future spiritual battle waged by a mother and her son, all creation had to wait for their appearance. It took a very long time. Life went on outside the Garden; God's plan was not to be thwarted. His intention in making man and woman in his image and likeness had always been to share with them his life and love. They were now flawed, having lost their original grace, yet God was not deterred.

There would be many more acts in this drama before its final one, the conclusion of human history within time. In the light of the New Testament, we read Genesis 3:15 as referring to Mary, so that we learn to expect a mother and son, but long before their appearance, there were "types" of them throughout the Old Testament, men and women who foreshadowed them in various ways. As we might expect from their iconic likeness to God, men have larger, more prominent roles than women in moving salvation history forward. However, we must remember that in the beginning God created both male and female to be images representing him in creation. That means that men and women, together, fulfill God's design.

The Woman, Eve

As St. John Paul II wrote, "Womanhood expresses the 'human' as much as manhood does ... It is only through the duality of the 'masculine' and the 'feminine' that the 'human' finds full realization."[8] With that in mind, let us think about Eve, the first woman in creation. What kind of woman was she? How did she get tangled up in the Serpent's trap? What became of her when she and Adam were expelled from the Garden? We will find that Eve's story does not end with her disobedience and shame. Prepare to be surprised.

When the Serpent began his conversation with Eve, he implied that God had put severe restrictions on what she and Adam were allowed to eat in the Garden: *"Did God say, 'You shall not eat of any tree of the garden'?"* (Genesis 3:1). Eve corrected him: *"We may eat of the fruit of the trees of the garden, but God said, 'You shall not eat of the fruit of the tree which is in the midst of the garden, neither shall you touch it, lest you die'"* (Genesis 3:2–3). Eve began her response with a defense of God's generosity, telling the Serpent that all the trees were theirs to eat from but one. Then, she reinforced the danger of eating from that one forbidden tree. She clearly understood what God had said.

We do wonder how the Serpent moved Eve from her noble rebuttal of his malicious twisting of God's words, where there is not even a whiff of doubt or rebellion, to reaching for the forbidden fruit. First, the Serpent contradicted God (*"you will not die,"* Genesis 3:4), suggesting that God had lied to her. This was the beginning of his cunning attack on God's character. Then, he directed her gaze to the fruit on that tree, while whispering all its benefits to her (*"you will be like God,"* Genesis 3:5). What he really meant, of course, was "you will be your own god," because in fact she and Adam were already like God, by his own creative intention. Eve's senses settled on all the fruit's appeal: it would be tasty; it was beautiful; it would make her wise. When she looked at the tree, she should have seen in its attractiveness the goodness of the One who created it (see also Romans 1:20; Wisdom 13:5). That did not happen. She did not ask God or Adam to help her know what to do.

Most of us are very familiar with the shadow that fell upon our first parents when Eve grasped that fruit and gave some to Adam. However, it was not all darkness. First, God made it very clear he was not about to give up on his human creation, as we have already noted. Then, he punished his disobedient children. God's punishments always come entirely from his love, as all parents know (see also Hebrews 12:3–11). We see with what care God himself clothed them when they were about to be expelled from the Garden: *"And the Lord God made for Adam and for his wife garments of skins and clothed them"* (Genesis 3:21). They had covered themselves with leaves; he covered them with animal skins. The leaves were the best that humans could muster, as insubstantial as they were. The animal skins God provided would protect and preserve them, the sure mark of his divine love.

Physical death would now be a part of man's existence, in addition to the spiritual death that happened in the Garden. Surely that seems harsh. We expect creatures who were meant to live forever, as God designed them, would experience it that way. Is there any hint that things were not as they seem in this dramatic turning point of man's story? Perhaps there is one— God did not destroy the Garden upon man's departure. He left it standing. The Tree of Life remained, with its fruit that could make man live forever. Angels with swords were stationed at its entrance to prevent Adam and Eve from returning. Would the rest of this story include man's return to the Garden someday in a radically changed condition and the ability to eat the life-giving fruit from a tree planted by God? The plot thickens ...

For now, we must go with Adam and Eve as they began life outside the Garden. God had given them his first commandment at the time of their creation: *"Be fruitful and multiply"* (Genesis 1:28). They were now ready to obey him. *"Adam knew Eve his wife, and she conceived and bore Cain"* (Genesis 4:1). Did they have a new respect for doing what God told them to do? If we keep a careful eye on Eve, we will find an answer.

When Cain was born, Eve made a simple statement: *"I have gotten a man with the help of the LORD"* (Genesis 4:1). At first glance, this might seem like predictable maternal commentary on the birth of her firstborn child. However, we remember Eve's choice of independence from both Adam and God as she reached for that forbidden fruit. She wanted to be her own god. Look at her now. She saw the birth of Cain as a *gift* from God. She acknowledged his help, his involvement with her *personally*. In the Garden, she grasped; outside the Garden, she received. Clearly, Eve had changed.

Although Eve had changed, she still experienced the consequences of what happened in the Garden. After Cain, she gave birth to Abel. She watched them grow, every mother's

delight. We come into their story again when they are older. We
see that although they were both raised by the same parents, in
the same way, and with the same lessons about God, they were
very different men. Abel took his parents' teaching and example
to heart. He was generous in his offering to God (see Genesis
4:3–7). Perhaps Cain was simply going through the motions,
doing what was expected of him and the bare minimum at that.
His heart was hard, and that hardness was obvious to God in the
offering he made. So, out of his desire to open Cain's heart, God
rejected his offering. He did not reject Cain, of course, but urged
him to "*do well*," putting everything right (see Genesis 4:7).

Instead of accepting God's invitation to change, Cain further
hardened his heart, allowing jealousy of Abel to provoke him
to murder. Then, wrapped in the darkness he had chosen for
himself, he refused to take responsibility for what he had done.
God had to send him away, expelling him from his family and
"*from the presence of the LORD*" (Genesis 4:16) forever. Imagine
what all of this might have meant to Eve. She had delighted in
the birth of Cain as a gift from God. Then she had to watch her
son slowly turn away from God into utter darkness. This kind of
turn does not usually happen overnight. It is a day-by-day pain
in the heart of any mother who sees it. Then, Cain murdered the
son who had responded so completely to God and his goodness.
What anguish this must have been for their mother, to lose both
sons at once, a suffering deeper than words can describe.

Suppose for a moment we could stop the action of this story
here. We might want to ask Eve what she thought *now* about the
goodness of God that had moved her to humble gratitude after
Cain's birth. We would be curious to see if she was still confident
in his kindness, his great plan for the future of human history,

in his trustworthiness. What might she say in answer to these questions? What might we say?

We can all understand what Eve might have felt because of what she suffered in this tragic twist in her life. Yet it is here we find a great surprise. *"And Adam knew his wife again, and she bore a son and called his name Seth, for she said, 'God has appointed for me another child instead of Abel, for Cain slew him'"* (Genesis 4:25). Once again, Eve acknowledged the kindness of God in giving her another son. This is a much-overlooked miraculous moment, coming so early in our human story. It is worth pondering.

After Cain killed Abel, Eve did not curse God and want to die herself. She didn't despair of life outside the Garden where horribly bad things can happen to good people. She saw Seth's birth as a gift from God to her *personally* to fill the void left by Abel. She could still see God's goodness through her veil of tears. She was still able to have hope for the future and thus be glad to birth another child. We ought to be curious about what could have given Eve this kind of courage. Remarkably, she was unafraid of the future, even though she knew firsthand what it might bring. Any of us who have known the pain of living through awful suffering, whatever the cause, will be interested in the answer to this question. We can only piece together the evidence, of course, but even that can be worthwhile. To do it, we will need to think very carefully about the woman, Eve.

- She was the only woman who has ever lived who saw with her own eyes the Garden of Eden untouched by the shadow of sin, just as it had come from God's hands.
- She and Adam experienced human communion with God as he walked in the Garden *"in the cool of the day"*

(see Genesis 3:8), the kind of communion humans will only fully know again in heaven.

- She knew, personally, the love of God that continued to enfold his human creatures even after their shocking rebellion. She and Adam were the first people ever to experience God's mercy.

From what she had learned about God, contrary to the Serpent's lies about him, Eve was able to continue to trust God and his plan. She saw God's good hand of comfort and provision in her great loss. Her voice was small, her words few, yet in great humility she became the first person in Scripture to feel the devastating consequences of sin, experiencing indescribable suffering, and answer it *only* with words of God's goodness to her. Let us hear what the *Catechism* says about God's love for this woman as it describes Jesus' descent into hell:

> The earth trembled and is still because God has fallen asleep in the flesh and he has raised up all who have slept ever since the world began. ... He has gone to search for Adam, our first father, as for a lost sheep ... he has gone to free from sorrow Adam in his bonds and Eve, captive with him—He who is both their God and the son of Eve. ..." I am your God, who for your sake have become your son. ... I order you, O sleeper, to awake. I did not create you to be a prisoner in hell. Rise from the dead, for I am the life of the dead." (CCC 635)

Eve and Mary

Eve, a type of Mary, helps us understand an important characteristic of Old Testament types, both men and women— they are types, not the realities toward which they point. This is true of both men and women who lived in the time before the appearance of the promised mother and son. We can experience real disappointment when we see that the types were flawed. As we explore the ways in which the Old Testament women who are types point to Mary, it is important to emphasize that Mary is above every other human being ever created. The fact is, all of us have a longing to see perfect people, even though we know we ourselves are far from perfect. This longing in man's heart may have begun in Eden, when God promised to send against his enemy just such a man and woman, perfect people in a state of grace, in full allegiance to him, and ready to fight on his side. Perhaps the longing is a sign in us, flawed as we are, that God's plan has always been our perfection. Jesus said as much when he told his followers, *"You, therefore, must be perfect, as your heavenly Father is perfect"* (Matthew 5:48). We need to be patient as we see how God works this plan to its conclusion.

How is Eve, flawed as she is, a type of Mary? In some ways, Eve can seem to be the exact opposite. She was a fallen woman, after all. However, if we do not grasp the beautiful, blessed grace of Eve, we will struggle to see why Mary, from the time of the early Church, has been seen by Christians as the New Eve. Glancing back at the story we have just heard will help us solve this dilemma.

Though never full of grace like Mary or as close to God as she was, both Adam and Eve were in a state of grace when they were created by God's hands. God breathed into Adam's nostrils *"the breath of life"* (Genesis 2:7). He made Eve from Adam's bone and flesh; she, too, was full of God's own breath. Adam and Eve lost their grace through disobedience, evident immediately in the shame they felt in their naked bodies, their desire to hide from God, and their reluctance to accept responsibility for their actions. God promised to send another man and woman, a mother and son, to defeat the Serpent. We ought to *expect* them both to be in a state of grace, as Adam and Eve once had been. In the beginning, a conversation a woman had with a fallen angel began the great drama of our human story. Many thousands of years later, in the story's new beginning, a conversation a woman in a perfect state of grace had with the angel Gabriel began an even greater dramatic moment in our story. The new story would tell of our redemption, the triumph over tragedy.

Mary is the New Eve because she was full of grace, God's original design for all women. When Gabriel greeted her with the words that are regularly on our lips, *"Hail, full of grace"* (Luke 1:28), he was not simply complimenting her. The Greek word for this phrase in St. Luke's Gospel is *kecharitomene*. It is in the past perfect tense, meaning that Mary had been and was then *already* graced; she was not simply about to receive grace. Her soul was full of divine life, just as Eve's had been when God fashioned her from Adam's rib. At the Fall, God promised a new start for his creation, one that would begin with a man and woman, as the first one had. These would have to be extraordinary people! All human descendants from our first parents, other than the promised man and woman, have been born tainted by Adam and Eve's disobedience, which we call original sin. We are no match for God's powerful angelic enemy, Satan.

Mary was born of human parents, but because of her unique vocation as the mother of Jesus, as the New Eve, God preserved her from the stain of original sin. This should not surprise us. As St. John Paul II once wrote,

Mary's pure and immaculate conception is thus seen as the beginning of the new creation. It is a question of a personal privilege granted to the woman chosen to be Christ's Mother, who ushers in the time of abundant grace God willed for all humanity ... Mary is full of sanctifying grace and was so from the first moment of her existence. This grace, according to Ephesians 1:3-6, is bestowed in Christ on all believers. Mary's original holiness represents the unsurpassable model of the gift and distribution of Christ's grace in the world.[9]

This idea was beautifully described in the eighth century by Andrew of Crete: "The Virgin's body is ground which God has tilled, the first fruits of Adam's soil divinized by Christ, the image truly like the former beauty, the clay kneaded by the divine artist."[10]

Our reading of Genesis 3:15 in the context of the New Testament shows how Eve helps us see that the new beginning for creation, the one God promised after the Fall, will start with a mother and son who were both full of grace. Eve opens our eyes to much more, too.

God created Eve to solve Adam's only problem in Eden before the Fall. *"It is not good that the man should be alone; I will make him a helper fit for him"* (Genesis 2:18). Man was created in God's image and likeness, so he must be in communion with another like himself. God is a Trinitarian communion, as we see when God says, *"Let us make man in our image, after our likeness"* (Genesis 1:26). There needed to be *"us"* in Eden. The animals provided companionship, but Adam needed more than that. Eve was the answer to Adam's need to live in the image and likeness of God. That is why he said, *"This at last is bone of my bones and flesh of my flesh"* (Genesis 2:23). As his wife, Eve would enable

Adam to be fruitful, to make other humans, male and female, just as God had done. She would also join him in having dominion over God's creation. In all this, hers would be the role of *helper*. This is a subordinate role, but the vocation to it was not a subordinate one.

Eve was a helper by God's design. What does that suggest about the mother to come, the one God promised at the Fall? She, too, would be a helper. If we understand this in the beginning, seeing Eve as a type of Mary, we will understand why Mary's role in the Gospel stories is small but not insignificant. She is not a dominant figure in all the action they record; her spoken words are scant. However, what matters is the meaning of her words and actions in Scripture, not their number. Eve, the helper fit for Adam, keeps us grounded in this great truth. She stood at the center of the dramatic moment in our history when a choice was required. It was a choice upon which the future of humanity would hinge. Eve was the first woman to be given a responsibility like this, but not the last. On a day that must have seemed ordinary in every other way, Mary would be given an equally powerful choice. Eve, even though she chose badly, is a type of Mary, who chose wisely. She foreshadows the moment when a woman, a helper, one in a subordinate role, would by her obedience to God undo the catastrophic consequences of Eve's disobedience.

Just like Mary after her, Eve faced a momentous choice that affected generations to come. Her very name foreshadows the name by which the new mother would be known throughout all generations. Adam named his wife Eve *"because she was the mother of all living"* (Genesis 3:20). Eve's biological relationship with all people who lived would be forever established in her exalted title, Mother of All Living. This helps us recognize what happened on Calvary: *"When Jesus saw his mother, and the disciple whom he loved standing near, he said to his mother, 'Woman, behold, your son!' Then he said to the disciple, 'Behold, your mother!'"* (John 19:26–27). Was Jesus, as a responsible son, simply tidying up the matter of Mary's care and comfort when he was gone? No, he was establishing a *spiritual* relationship between his mother and all his followers, starting with the faithful St. John standing at the foot of the Cross. Many years after the Crucifixion, St. John had a heavenly vision of the great battle between the archangel Michael and the dragon who tried to destroy the woman and the child born of her, *"the male child, one who is to rule all the nations"* (Revelation 12:5). In it, he described this woman as mother not only to that *"male child"* but also mother to *"the rest of her offspring ... those who keep the commandments of God and bear testimony to Jesus"* (Revelation 12:17). The woman is known to us by an exalted title, as was Eve—Mary, Mother of God and, by his gift, the Church's own mother, too. Just as God gave Eve another son to comfort her heart and continue her vocation as mother, so Mary received another son, as well as all those who love Jesus, to comfort her heart and continue her vocation as mother.

Finally, outside of Eden, Eve was able to understand her true posture before God and was able to receive, not grasp, what God wanted to give her. Years later, when Gabriel announced God's plan to Mary, she responded, *"Let it be to me according to your word"* (Luke 1:38). Mary's answer restored the vocation of women, to receive from God his blessing and gifts. What Eve had inverted, Mary set right side up. May her response resound first on the lips of all women and then through all creation.

— Pondering Eve —

Perhaps as we have slowly pondered the details of Eve's life recorded for us in Genesis, we have found ourselves learning something from her. Here are a few questions to help you continue finding ways that Eve's life can speak to you:

When Eve was tempted to doubt God's goodness and to act contrary to his command, she did not call out to God or Adam for help. She acted all on her own.

- Have there been times when you know you should have prayed or asked for help but did not? If so, what were the results?
- What situations tempt you to act without first praying for God's direction?

Eve was distracted from obeying God's command by the beauty and benefits of the forbidden fruit.

- Is now a good time to check yourself for distractions that are not bad in themselves but have kept you away from attention to your relationship with God or other people?

Eve learned lessons about herself and God through her experience of disobeying him. These lessons changed her in a wonderful way. They replaced the pride of her grasping at fruit in the Garden with the humility of receiving the fruit of her womb as God's gift to her.

- What lessons like these have you learned through your failures?
- What simple prayer can you put on your lips today to keep these lessons alive for you when you most need them?

Being plunged into heart-crushing suffering, either our own or that of others, can shake our confidence in God to its foundations. There is a whisper inside of us: *How could God let this happen to us if he loves us?* Surely both Eve and Mother Mary were acquainted with this kind of great sorrow. However, they both persevered. They had experienced the reality of God's profoundly personal love for them before their suffering arrived. They trusted that his love would continue, no matter what.

- Is your life now being touched by the kind of suffering that makes you want to question the goodness of God and his care for us? If so, perhaps these words from St. Catherine of Siena can help you regain your confidence:

Our heart should burst right out of our body at the realization of the status and dignity to which infinite Goodness has appointed us—first by creating us in his own image, and then by joining his divine nature with our humanity to ransom us and create us anew! More than this he could not give: to give himself to those who by sin had become his enemies. O ineffable, consummate love! You really are in love with what you have made![11]

Can you let the example of these three women—Eve, Mother Mary, St. Catherine—nourish your soul and strengthen it to trust that no matter how things look or feel, God really is in love with what he has made—you and all of us? They teach us to reject the Serpent's lie about God, his whisper that tells us God is not on our side. We know we can trust him.

- Are there any lingering impressions from Eve's life that you do not want to forget? Perhaps you can write them down here or in your own journal.

* Father Robert Spitzer (reconciles Science with Faith)

Chapter Two

Sarah—In the Time of the Patriarchs

"God has made laughter for me."

–Genesis 21:6

Historical Context: Patriarchs (2200–1800 BC)

God's first family, Adam and Eve with their offspring, was fractured by sin and its consequences. Cain, who murdered his brother Abel, was sent away from the presence of the Lord. Both he and Seth, the son God gave Eve to replace Abel, formed families of their own. Seth and his descendants *"began to call on the name of the LORD"* (Genesis 4:26) the way Adam and Eve must have taught them to do. Cain and his family, however, were full of violence, both physical and moral. Eventually, this evil polluted nearly all there was of the human race. Such is the insatiable appetite of sin. When *"the LORD saw that the wickedness of man was great in the earth and that every imagination of the thoughts of his heart was only evil continually"* (Genesis 6:5), he decided to wash the earth clean and start over with the one righteous man on it, Noah. He sent the Flood, sparing Noah and his family, along with all the animals they had taken with them into the Ark. That, however, did not rid the human soul of sin. Sin grew again, symbolized in the building of the Tower of Babel—an unforgettable expression of man's intention to grasp at heaven by his own wits. God struck down this attempt, confusing the one language men had spoken into many. This confusion would have made it harder for them to communicate evil intentions to each other, thus restraining sin's contagious power.

There was one family on earth, descendants of Noah's oldest son, Shem, who still had a rudimentary knowledge of God and the covenant he made with Noah after the Flood. God chose one member of this family, Abram (later to become Abraham), to form a nation to be his very own.

With the call of Abram, the era of the Early World comes to an end, and the era of the Patriarchs begins. God would reveal himself more fully to this one nation descended from Abraham, teaching them how to live in harmony with his original design for man. They, in turn, could teach the other nations on the earth, thus reconciling man with God. In about 2200 BC, God called Abram; his wife was named Sarai (later to become Sarah).

The Woman, Sarah

Sarah is a woman whom Jews, all throughout their history, have revered as the mother of God's covenant people. The Jewish Christians among the New Testament writers look back on her with admiration, seeing her as a godly woman and a great example of faith (see Hebrews 11:11; 1 Peter 3:5–6). We want to examine her story to see why.

When we first meet Sarah, her name is Sarai, and we learn early on that she is barren. Although she and Abram came from a wealthy family and could live comfortably, *"she had no child"* (Genesis 11:30). We can imagine what barrenness meant in a time when having large families was vital to existence. Even in our own day, women suffering from infertility bear testimony to how it can strike a searing blow to a woman's identity, robbing her of her heart's deepest desire. We also know that Sarai was remarkably beautiful (Genesis 12:11). Think of this combination—barren and beautiful. We might wonder how she experienced both. Her barrenness could have soured her on the joy that her beauty could give others. All of us, male or female, find pleasing satisfaction in seeing a physically beautiful person. However, although she could not give her husband a child, Abram seems to have had no desire for other wives. He must have found contentment in their marriage, suggesting that her barrenness had not embittered her. Perhaps her beauty softened the pain of her empty womb, giving her some comfort in the delight it gave her husband and others.

Although Sarai and Abram lived with their extended family in Ur of the Chaldeans, their father, Terah (they had the same father but different mothers), decided to move all of them to the land of Canaan. Some have suggested that he was pursuing an ancestral right to that land. They stopped on the way in Haran, settling there. That may have been because of Terah's poor health; he died there. It was there, in Haran, that God spoke to Abram, calling him to a future he could hardly imagine. To know Sarai, we need to know this call to her husband, recounted in Genesis 12.

> "Now the LORD said to Abram, 'Go from your country and your kindred and your father's house to the land that I will show you. And I will make of you a great nation, and I will bless you, and make your name great, so that you will be a blessing. I will bless those who bless you, and him who curses you I will curse; and by you all the families of the earth shall bless themselves'" (Genesis 12:1–3).

There are several parts to this call, but we can see there is a certain dynamic movement in it. God's call for Abram to go forth from home and family was aimed at making him a source of universal blessing. We hear the Lord tell Abram, *"By you all the families of the earth shall bless themselves."* Abram would receive many blessings: a land that would become home for him and his descendants and the promise of a great nation to come from him, one that would include dynastic kings. The blessings were all intended to bless others. We need to keep this in mind.

Think about the conversation Abram and Sarai might have had when he told her about this remarkable call from God to them. When Sarai heard it, we can imagine what part of it would have immediately gotten her attention: God would make of her husband *"a great nation."* That meant offspring! Wonder of wonders, she and Abram would begin a family that would eventually grow into a dynastic nation. We can be confident that, even with the difficulty and pain of leaving home and family for a land unknown to them, they were eager to do what God asked them to do. Why would they hesitate when the reward was so great?

When they first arrived in Canaan, in a place called Shechem, God spoke to Abram again, renewing his promise to give the land to his descendants (see Genesis 12:7–8). Abram's response was to build *"there an altar to the Lord."* Then, they moved on to a place near Bethel, where Abram pitched their tent, built another altar, *"and called on the name of the Lord."* The altars tell us something about how Abram and Sarai understood what was happening in their lives. Certainly they must have felt apprehensive about all the unknown in this move. It could be that at those altars, Abram and Sarai not only thanked God for his marvelous promises but also asked for his protection and help for all that lay ahead. And God's help was exactly what they would need.

When they discovered that the land God had given them was devastated by a terrible famine, Abram decided to go to Egypt, where there was a high, cultured civilization and no famine. The idea was not in itself bad, but one important element was missing in his plan. He did not ask God about it, and that led to trouble.

When they got to Egypt, Abram worried that Sarai's great beauty would attract the attention of the Pharaoh, so he asked her to say they were brother and sister, a half-truth, not husband and wife. He believed this would preserve his life; she agreed to do it. We know from what happened later in her story that she was not a woman afraid to speak her mind, yet there is no word of objection recorded here. That must have been because she also feared for Abram's life and was willing to do anything, even something as difficult and unpleasant as this must have been for both, to protect him. So, Sarai went into the Pharaoh's household, and Abram was richly repaid for letting her go. Their intentions in all this were good, but good intentions did not spare them the consequences of a bad plan.

Once Sarai became part of the Pharaoh's harem, God struck his house with terrible plagues. This let Pharaoh know something was terribly wrong in his household. He soon discovered what Abram and Sarai had done, information he likely could get only from Sarai herself. He was furious, incredulous over how Abram could do such a thing. We wonder, if a pagan king could see how wrong this plan was, why couldn't Abram and Sarai? Apparently, they had been blinded by their desperation. Providentially, God reached down to save them both, teaching them something they truly needed to absorb—they could trust God with their lives.

The Pharaoh sent them packing, of course, and they had a decision to make. They were now quite wealthy with the king's gifts to them. Should they give up on this wild call of God and return to the safety and comfort of Haran? Or should they return to Canaan, where an uncertain future awaited them? Although Abram was wealthy after his stay in Egypt, *"he journeyed on from the Negeb as far as Bethel, to the place where his tent had been at the beginning, between Bethel and Ai, to the place where he had made an altar at the first; and there Abram called on the name of the Lord"* (Genesis 13:3–4). They chose to believe the promises of God. They had learned something from the mess they created living by their own wits. It was better to be where God called them, even with famine, than to live in luxury outside of God's will. They made a fresh start.

Before we leave this episode, we want to remember that God took the initiative to rescue these foolish people. He did the same thing in Eden. He did not interfere with their freedom to choose badly, but when they experienced the painful consequences, he cared for them when they most needed him. This truth about God's love for us has been consistently evident from the dawn of creation. It forms a pattern appearing throughout salvation history. It culminated in the Incarnation, when God became one of us to free us from the mess we had made of ourselves. As the Church prays every year in the Easter Exultet, "O wonder of your humble care for us! O love, O charity beyond all telling, to ransom a slave you gave away your Son!"[12] Exactly.

After Abram and Sarai returned to Canaan, seemingly more confident they could trust God, they encountered another challenge to that trust—the test of time. Ten years passed without the birth of a child, and the long wait took its toll on both of them. In their impatience and exasperation, they each made plans to get what they wanted—an heir to begin the fulfillment of the promises God had made. Abram wanted to make a servant in their home his heir (see Genesis 15:2). God listened and then simply said, *"This man shall not be your heir; your own son shall be your heir"* (Genesis 15:4). Sarai, too, was deep into self-pity, a cancer that had eaten away at her trust in God. As Scripture says in Proverbs, *"Hope deferred makes the heart sick"* (Proverbs 13:12). When she could stand it no longer, Sarai told Abram, *"Behold now, the LORD has prevented me from bearing children"* (Genesis 16:2). Her pain drove her to blame God for the problem, and she accused him of "preventing" her from getting pregnant. So, she suggested to him that he resort to a custom common at that time, to use Sarai's servant, Hagar, to give her the child she desperately wanted. They could be done with all the waiting on God, and Abram agreed.

Not surprisingly, Sarai's plan produced disaster. Hagar bore Abram's child, Ishmael, and then she *"looked with contempt on her mistress"* (Genesis 16:4). That infuriated Sarai, and in the heat of her anger she blamed Abram for the mess: *"May the wrong done to be me on you!"* (Genesis 16:5). Abram passively excused himself from all responsibility: *"Your maid is in your power; do to her as you please"* (Genesis 16:6). Sarai dealt harshly with her, so Hagar fled. What had looked like a good plan to give Sarai what she wanted only gave her what she did not want—discord with her husband. Eventually, Hagar returned to Abram and Sarai by God's direction and help. Abram raised Ishmael and loved him as his firstborn son. Although this calmed his household and gave him the joy of fatherhood, a seed of discontent had been planted. Someday it would bear bitter fruit.

When Abram was ninety-nine years old, God appeared to him, renewing all his promises and establishing the sign of the covenant—circumcision—that would identify him and all his descendants as his very own people. Both he and Sarai got new names to indicate the bright future that lay ahead for them. Abram became *"Abraham,"* meaning the *"father of a multitude of nations"* (Genesis 17:5), and Sarai became *"Sarah,"* for she would be the *"mother of nations; kings of peoples shall come from her"* (Genesis 17:16). God also promised that in a year's time, Sarah would give birth to a son, to be named "Isaac" (see Genesis 17:19), meaning "he laughs." Why such an unusual name? After all, there was nothing funny about how long his parents had to wait for him. God gave Abraham's son this name because when he heard God's timetable for the birth of this long-delayed son, he fell on his face laughing and asked instead if all God's promises could be realized through Ishmael. Abraham still struggled to believe God could work a miracle like that in their aging bodies.

So did Sarah. Later, three angelic messengers appeared one day at their camp. While Sarah was in the tent, she heard, through the voice of God's messenger, a renewal of his promise of a son. Sarah was past childbearing age,

> so Sarah laughed to herself, saying, *"After I have grown old, and my husband is old, shall I have pleasure?"* The LORD said to Abraham, *"Why did Sarah laugh, and say, 'Shall I indeed bear a child, now that I am old?' Is anything too hard for the LORD? At the appointed time I will return to you, in the spring, and Sarah shall have a son."* But Sarah denied, saying, *"I did not laugh"; for she was afraid. He said, "No, but you did laugh."* (Genesis 18:12–15)

Sarah laughed to herself with disbelief. She simply could not imagine that God could do such an impossible thing. The angelic messenger who heard the laugh understood what caused it. He chided her, asking, "*Is anything too hard for the* Lord*?*" Then, she made matters worse and lied about laughing, but the angel knew better.

After the angelic messengers left, Sarah had time to think about what they had told her and how she reacted to it. Did she regret that impulsive laugh? Did the memory of its sound haunt her? If Sarah thought back over the long life she had lived with God, she would perhaps have realized that he had, indeed, been good to her and Abraham. Even in her personal lapses of faith, God continued to care for them in the land he had given them. If she thought back to her laughing outburst, going over the whole exchange word-for-word (as we often do when we have serious regrets about our behavior), perhaps she was able to focus on what she should have heard in the first place in the angel's message. He sounded confident about the birth of that baby, giving them a specific time, "*in the spring,*" for his birth. He also pinpointed the exact cause of her laugh—she *did* believe there was something "*too hard for the* Lord*.*" Did she cringe when she realized how foolish that was? If so, we can let ourselves think that out of that dark moment in her life with God, hope in his promises was reborn in her.

We wish we could have watched Sarah when the first unmistakable signs of her pregnancy appeared in her body. Inexpressible joy! As her body grew larger, perhaps her loving trust in God did as well. When Isaac was born, all this bubbled up out of her: *And Sarah said, 'God has made laughter for me; every one who hears will laugh over me'* (Genesis 21:6). She finally understood that all along God wanted laughter for her and Abraham. Now, theirs would be the delightful, infectious laughter over the miracle of God doing the utterly impossible for them. The cynical laugh in her darkest moment had been transformed into a laugh she expected all who heard her story would share. Sarah, with all her stumbles, is the first person in Scripture to express the awe and wonder that any of us who have been touched by God's transforming love are able to share: "*God has made laughter for me.*"

Sarah's story includes another episode involving Hagar; it requires our attention (see Genesis 21:9–14). When Isaac was probably about three years old, Abraham and Sarah held a great feast to celebrate his weaning. Sarah noticed Ishmael "*playing*" with Isaac. St. Paul, in the New Testament, describes this episode: "*he who was born according to the flesh* [Ishmael] *persecuted him who was born according to the Spirit* [Isaac]" (Galatians 4:28–31). Perhaps he was mocking Isaac, laughing at him about being a "big boy" but not the biggest, not the firstborn as he was. Sarah spoke strongly to Abraham about this: "*Cast out this slave woman with her son; for the son of this slave woman shall not be heir with my son Isaac*" (Genesis 21:10). This might look like Sarah's ugly return to her old form with Hagar. However, because of Sarah's deeper conversion to the Lord when Isaac was born, she was now a changed woman. Earlier, she treated Hagar harshly to protect herself from Hagar's disrespectful, contemptuous attitude. This time, Sarah's concern was to protect her son's rightful, God-given position as the sole inheritor of all the promises God had made to Abraham and his descendants. Sarah was probably aware that Abraham's tender affection for the boy made him vulnerable to forgetting that distinction (see Genesis 21:11). More importantly, this time Abraham consulted God about what to do. God had a remarkable response to it. We are told: *"But God said to Abraham, 'Be not displeased because of the lad and because of your slave woman; whatever Sarah says to you, do as she tells you, for through Isaac shall your descendants be named'"* (Genesis 21:12). This time, Sarah was speaking God's own wisdom to her husband.

Finally, in the long story of Sarah's life, there is one more very familiar episode, but there is no record of her involvement in or reaction to it in Scripture. In fact, there is complete silence from Sarah when God told Abraham to sacrifice Isaac (see Genesis 22:1–2). That raises questions.

First, we wonder if Abraham told Sarah about God's frightening call to him. It could have been one of those "don't tell Mom" episodes that can happen in family life. However, we know that from the time of her deeper conversion, Sarah was a woman of faith who believed God would keep his promises. Abraham had heard God speak to him through Sarah before. It seems very likely he would have discussed something as unexpected and confusing as this with her. Perhaps they stayed up all night talking it through. By the time dawn was breaking, they knew what they had to do. Sarah, as the helper God had given Abraham, very likely encouraged him, for he surely would have needed it. She would have reminded him of all God's faithfulness to them. They both knew that nothing was too hard for the Lord; somehow this would all work out. Then, *"early in the morning,"* she let him and her son go (Genesis 22:3).

After that, silence descended for Sarah. Her silence probably came from the same source as Abraham's silence. When God told him to sacrifice Isaac, he said nothing (see Genesis 22:1–2). This silence is not hard to understand. To be thunderstruck by something enormous, when God's will seems to mean the death of dreams, there are no words. What were those hours that turned into three days like for Sarah? She would need to believe that no matter what happened, God was willing and able to keep all his promises. Her memory would have to bring alive again the sound of her joyous laughter at Isaac's birth, when she knew firsthand that God delights in surprising us with what he can do. She might have needed to repeat her son's name over and over—"Isaac, he laughs"—to hold herself steady. She would have to remember that her laughter came at the end of oceans of tears, that it burst forth from her when she realized that God had worked an unthinkable reversal for her. All her hopes would have rested on that. Pope Benedict XVI once wrote, "Jesus is Isaac, who, risen from the dead, comes down from the mountain with the laughter of joy on his face. All the words of the Risen One manifest this joy—this laughter of redemption: if you see what I see and have seen ... you will laugh!"[13]

In due time, three days later, Sarah did see her son approaching with Abraham on the horizon. We can imagine that glorious homecoming.

Sarah and Mary

If all we knew about Sarah was that she is the mother of God's Old Covenant people, we might think her role as a type of Mary was small, though significant. Mary became the mother of God's New Covenant people. Sarah, to become that mother, gave birth miraculously to a son whom God promised her. Mary gave birth miraculously to a Son whom God promised her. That alone establishes Sarah as one of the Old Testament types of Mary. We, however, know more about Sarah than that she was Isaac's mother. What, then, does her life suggest to us about the mother she foreshadowed?

The details of Sarah's life span many years, perhaps more than any other woman's story in the Old Testament. She and Abraham had a lot to learn about living with faith and trust in God. They made mistakes. Yet they did not give up on God, and he did not give up on them. Their lives were difficult; the long wait for a child of their own was not easy. For Sarah, in whose body the miracle was supposed to take place, there must have been a subterranean current of doubt in her that was impossible to completely cut off. She daily experienced the toll of time that none of us can avoid as we grow older. It is no surprise that when she heard the angelic messenger who visited their camp say, as clear as a bell, that it was going to happen, all the doubt that had taken up residence in her body found expression in a laugh so loud it could be heard outside the tent, and that laugh changed everything.

At the critical moment in her life, when she simply had to believe in what was physically impossible, the angel put the choice before her: *"Is anything too hard for the Lord?"* That is a question that cannot be ignored. Sarah surely had to think about it. With slow and halting steps, did she begin making her way to an answer? She did not have to wait long. In three months, the body that had for so many years insisted to her that the miracle could never happen became the body that left no doubt it could.

At the time when Gabriel visited her, Mary also had to believe that the miracle of birth would take place in her body. The challenge for her was not barrenness and age; it was her virginity. She asked, *"How can this be, since I have no husband?"* (Luke 1:34). Mary did not doubt that God could do the impossible, but she was certainly curious about *how* it would happen. Gabriel explained it to her and then gently told her the news of Elizabeth's miraculous pregnancy: *"For with God, nothing will be impossible"* (Luke 1:37). He must have thought that knowing about Elizabeth would encourage her. When Mary heard his words, did she think of Sarah and remember her laugh of pure delight over this truth? Confident that God would do the impossible in her, as he had done in both Sarah and Elizabeth, she responded to Gabriel: *"I am the handmaid of the Lord; let it be to me according to your word"* (Luke 1:38).

The joy that filled Sarah's heart and mind at Isaac's birth found expression in the laughter that has resounded through all the ages that lived after her. She said, *"Every one who hears will laugh over me"* (Genesis 21:6). Sarah knew that anyone hearing her story of God's goodness to her would rejoice and call her blessed, for truly she was. Mary was the mother Sarah foreshadowed, and when her heart and mind were full of the joy of God's miracle in her, Mary sang out, *"All generations will call me blessed"* (Luke 1:48). Mary was confident that the story of God's mercy and favor on her would inspire all those who heard it to marvel and call her blessed. Her vision is fulfilled every day, around the world, on countless lips that repeat what she knew so well: *"Blessed are you among women"* (Luke 1:42).

Finally, Sarah had to wait three days to see what happened after Abraham took Isaac away to sacrifice him to God as he had been told to do. The New Testament tells us that Abraham was able to do this because *"he considered that God was able to raise men even from the dead"* (Hebrews 11:19). Perhaps Sarah, on the night before he left, helped him to that kind of faith by reminding him of the angelic messenger's piercing question: *"Is anything too hard for the* LORD*?"* Sarah, as she waited in her silent vigil, likely had to remind herself, too. As it turned out, they *"did receive* [Isaac] *back, and this was a symbol"* (Hebrews 11:19).

Mary had to wait three days to see what would happen after her son's dead body was taken down from the Cross. In her silent vigil, did she think of what Sarah's vigil had been like? Even in her profound sorrow as a mother over what Jesus had suffered, could Mary look forward to his return, which Isaac's return to Sarah had symbolized?

Sarah's life gives us in simple outlines the life we have come to know and love in Mary, the mother of the Messiah. We can let ourselves imagine that on the day of the Resurrection, Mary might have whispered to herself, *"God has made laughter for me."*

All Jewish women in Mary's day knew the story of Sarah, the renowned mother of God's covenant people. We have thought about how Mary might have pondered what she knew about Sarah in some critical moments in her life. Perhaps we can do that, too.

"Is anything too hard for the LORD?"

- Mary, like Sarah, heard an angel say that nothing is impossible for God. Is there something in your life with God now that makes you need to hear that, too? We might have relationships that have been broken and troubled for a long time. Is it possible God could heal them? We may have financial problems that haunt us every day. Is it possible for God to keep us safe? We may be lonely from living alone. Is it possible for God to comfort us and give us peace?
- The list could go on, for we all have times when we wonder if we can count on God. When they arrive, it is good to hear again in our hearts and minds what the angel asked Sarah: *"Is anything too hard for the LORD?"* Both Sarah and Mary can help us know the answer.

"Everyone who hears will laugh over me"

Mary, like Sarah, wanted to share with all who came after her the joy of God's mercy and goodness to her. They both recognized that the meaning of what God had done for them was far too wonderful to be exhausted by just one generation.

- Can we examine our lives to find what God has done for us that we know was nearly too good to be true? Have we been baptized in Christ, blessed with the gift of the Holy Spirit, initiated into the Body of Christ? If so, then anyone hearing of that would call us blessed. Has God answered any of our prayers in ways that delighted us and made us laugh? Then we are truly blessed. Have we suffered greatly with pain that seemed to consume us, only to find that Jesus comforted and healed us beyond what we imagined possible? Then blessed are we among women if we never forget God's personal goodness to us.

"God has made laughter for me."

Sarah had to face the possibility of Isaac's death, the worst pain a mother can ever know. Mary lived through the actual death of her own treasured son. She knew Sarah was reunited with Isaac; she knew she would be reunited with Jesus. He had told even his Apostles of his resurrection after death, but that went right over their heads. We can expect Mary heard him say it, too, piercing her soul with sorrow, then lifting it again with hope. It surely would not have been lost on her.

Still, for both Sarah and Mary, there were three days of pain, the kind that words cannot adequately describe. Yet both women experienced the truth of what Jesus taught in the Sermon on the Mount: "*Blessed are those who mourn, for they shall be comforted*" (Matthew 5:4).

- Is there mourning in your life right now? Is there a pain so unbearable that it takes your breath away? Can you be comforted and encouraged by Sarah and Mary that someday God will turn your tears into the laughter of joy? "*May those who sow in tears reap with shouts of joy!*" (Psalm 126:5).

Are there any lingering impressions from Sarah's life that you do not want to forget? Perhaps you can write them down here or in your own journal.

....

....

....

....

....

....

....

....

....

....

Chapter Three

Miriam—In the Time of Egypt and Exodus and the Desert Wanderings

"Sing to the Lord, for he has triumphed gloriously."
—Exodus 15:21

Historical Context: Egypt and Exodus (1800–1446 BC)

From Abraham and Sarah came a family that eventually grew into twelve tribes, each headed by one of the sons of Jacob, Isaac's son. Their stories are varied; some of them make us marvel that these people were really going to be God's very own. There was, however, one bright light among them—Joseph, Jacob's favorite son. His brothers were jealous of him and took an opportunity, when their father was not there to stop them, to get rid of him. They did not kill him, although they gave that some thought. Instead, they sold him as a slave to a traveling caravan headed to Egypt. God was always with Joseph; the brightness of his life, even though full of suffering and difficulties, marks him as one of the most beautiful types of Jesus in the Old Testament. After Joseph was carted away, his brothers convinced Jacob a wild animal had killed him. Years later, a great famine hit. In desperation, some of the brothers decided to go to Egypt to buy food. By God's guiding hand, they met Joseph again, who had risen to great power and reputation there. Eventually, the brothers were reconciled to him, with Joseph repeatedly comforting them over their previous sin against him: *"You meant evil against me; but God meant it for good"* (Genesis 50:20). He invited the whole family to come live in Egypt, where they were given fertile land and were respected as Joseph's relatives.

So the era of the Patriarchs ends, and the era of Egypt and Exodus begins. For, after many years of living in Egypt, a Pharaoh arose who disregarded the history of the Israelites and made slaves of them. Their bondage was very cruel, but instead of decreasing their numbers, they were ever more fruitful. The Pharaoh was so provoked by this miraculous increase that he ordered a severe punishment: *"Every son that is born to the Hebrews you shall cast into the Nile"* (Exodus 1:22). He was convinced that would solve his problem. He could not foresee how that would open the door to a much bigger problem for Pharaoh and all of Egypt.

The Woman, Miriam

Miriam's story begins when she was a young Hebrew girl living in Egypt during the time when her people were persecuted as slaves. She is best known as the sister of Moses, who became the great deliverer of the Israelites. When we first meet Miriam, however, she takes center stage as the one who helped deliver Moses, then her baby brother. She and her mother, Jochebed, devised a courageous plan they hoped would save the life of this three-month old boy, who was under Pharaoh's death sentence. They put him into a small basket they had turned into a boat and *"placed it among the reeds at the river's brink"* (Exodus 2:3). Perhaps they both knew that this was a spot where Pharaoh's daughter regularly bathed in the river. If so, they could hope that she or one of her servants would see the child and rescue him. Miriam *"stood at a distance, to know what would be done to him"* (Exodus 2:4).

The plan worked! When Pharaoh's daughter saw the basket and opened it, she knew the baby boy was a Hebrew child. She knew her father wanted babies like him dead, but his beauty and his helpless cry softened her heart. Miriam must have read the emotion on her face, seeing her kind pity, and she seized her moment. Thinking quickly, she asked Pharaoh's daughter, *"Shall I go and call you a nurse from the Hebrew women to nurse the child for you?"* (Exodus 2:7). We wonder if Pharaoh's daughter smiled at this scene—she finds the endangered baby, then immediately a young girl pops up out of the reeds asking if she needs a nursemaid. She must have realized this was no accident, but she did not care. She let Miriam fetch Jochebed, who received her boy back into her arms to nurse and love, possibly for as much as three years. Then, when he was weaned, she returned him to Pharaoh's daughter, *"and he became her son"* (Exodus 2:10).

It had taken some courage for Miriam to speak so boldly to Pharaoh's daughter. She likely had no idea what the response would be. She and her family had seriously disobeyed Pharaoh's command. Would they all suffer the consequences? The Pharaoh was ruthless in his hatred of the Hebrews. She must have considered the cost and decided it was a risk worth taking to preserve her brother's life. Perhaps, because of the boy's remarkable beauty, Miriam and Jochebed shared a conviction that, in some way, this boy was special to God. Theirs had been a devout family, of the tribe of Levi (later to become the only tribe not to apostatize with the golden calf at Mount Sinai). When their plan succeeded so miraculously, they must have been convinced they were right. We can imagine that in the several years in which Jochebed nursed Moses, she told him in simple, tender words that he was God's gift to her and, perhaps, to all God's people.

We do not know how much contact Moses had with his birth family once they returned him to the royal palace. We do know that when he became a man, he had a strong sense of connection with his people, the Hebrews (see Exodus 2:11). He did not simply become an Egyptian. This suggests the possibility that he did have occasional visits with his family. Perhaps they kept alive in his mind that he was special to God, that he might be in a position someday to help his people escape from their miserable bondage. One fateful day, Moses acted on that impulse to stop Egyptian injustice against them. It was disastrous; he became a murderer and a fugitive from justice. He fled Egypt, and whatever dream he may have had about helping his people died on the spot (see Exodus 2:11–15).

Many years later, when God called Moses to the mission he was born to carry out, it was in a way he could never have imagined when he lived in the royal court. God gave him the help of his brother, Aaron, to miraculously deliver the Israelites from Egypt. Miriam, whom Scripture never describes as married or a mother, also had a role in this great event, as the prophet Micah once described: *"For I* [God] *brought you up from the land of Egypt, and redeemed you from the house of bondage; and I set before you Moses, Aaron, and Miriam"* (Micah 6:4). She was the first woman in salvation history to be in leadership this way. What kind of leader was she?

The memorable scene of the young girl at the river, working to save her brother, gives us some hints. First, we recognized her courage. The value of trying to save the baby's life was greater to her than saving her own. If she believed she was serving God's plan, not just her own family's love for him, she must have known she had to speak up, to step out of hiding in the reeds, to expose herself to whatever might happen. These same qualities must have matured with her as she grew into an adult. To help Moses and Aaron deliver God's people, an exceedingly dangerous mission, would require all of them: courage, a tender heart for the Hebrews (they were a grumbling, complaining lot), and faith that God was with them.

Miriam, as a young girl, watched as Moses was delivered from the waters of a river to live a completely new life. Many years later, she watched an even greater rescue from water, this time as the Israelites fled their Egyptian enemies through the waters of the Red Sea. As Tim Gray and Jeff Cavins point out in their book *Walking with God*, "Miriam, who watched her brother float down the Nile and into the arms of Pharaoh's daughter and redemption, now sees Moses saved once again from death through water."[14] Not surprisingly, it was at this moment that we see the flowering of Miriam's gifts, both of leadership and prophecy (see Exodus 15:20–21). She is the first woman in salvation history whom we know as a prophetess (meaning one who speaks for God). Her feminine voice rang out in the wilderness as she led the other women in singing God's praises. This was a significant moment for God's people; it calls us to ponder it.

> "Then Miriam, the prophetess, took a timbrel in her hand; and all the women went out after her with timbrels and dancing. And Miriam sang to them: 'Sing to the Lord, for he has triumphed gloriously; the horse and his rider he has thrown into the sea." (Exodus 15:20–21)

We have heard feminine voices already in Scripture, from Eve and Sarah, but we have not heard a feminine voice sing praise of God. Miriam's is the first; it will not be our last. We see in this episode the same initiative in Miriam that we first witnessed at the Nile. There, she recognized her moment and acted on it. Here, she knew the hearts and minds of God's people were bursting with gratitude, relief, and joy. They were finally free! She knew they needed to give expression to all this, so she grabbed a timbrel (an ancient Israelite tambourine), called out to the women to follow her, and then led them in a physical and emotional celebration of God's mighty deliverance.

There is still more to see in this moment, as Fr. Damasus Winzen, OSB, writes in his book *Pathways in Scripture*. About the singing of both men and women, under the direction of Moses and Miriam, he says: "This is the hour when the Divine Office is born. The joy of salvation must find its expression in the liturgy, meaning the common, public worship of God's people." He goes on to connect the singing of God's people in the Old Testament to that of the people in Revelation chapter 15 verse 3, saying, "We see that the ultimate purpose of salvation is the glorification of God through his people."[15]

The women of the Old Testament give feminine voice to this truth over and over, beginning with Miriam. We all, men and women, continue it now during Mass when, after the Penitential Rite, we burst into singing the *Gloria*—"Glory to God in the highest!" We should be singing this with the same depth of gratitude and joy for our deliverance from sin, death, and the Devil as the Israelites did when they stood on the shore of the sea and saw the dead bodies of their enemies. We are free at last!

Historical Context: Desert Wanderings (1446–1406 BC)

After the Israelites crossed the Red Sea, they traveled to Mount Sinai, where God gave Moses the Ten Commandments and came down on the mountain to visit his people. In a great ceremony there, the people were sealed with blood from animal sacrifices into a covenant with God. Although the Israelites promised to do all that God required in his law, they broke that promise in short order. While Moses was up on the mountain with God getting directions for their liturgical worship, the people rebelled with the worship of a golden calf, giving up on both God and Moses to care for them. They were punished, but because of Moses' intercession for them, God agreed to continue to be their God as they made their journey to the Promised Land, Canaan. However, this time was marked by much murmuring against God and Moses. It eventually culminated in the people's refusal to enter Canaan when they reached its border. Ten of the twelve spies Moses sent to check the land came back with a chilling report to the people: impossible! They described the Canaanites as being big and powerful; compared to them, the spies felt like grasshoppers. The people were so terrified they refused to enter, even after two of the spies exhorted them to have faith in God for the victory. God gave them what they wanted. They wandered in the desert for forty years until that rebellious generation died off. It is during this time of discontent with God and Moses before they arrived at Canaan, the era of Desert Wanderings, that we meet Miriam again.

Her lesson for us here is quite different from her earlier one. Miriam gives us an example of how something good—

being gifted to be a leader among women—can expose us to a temptation, one to which she succumbed. As the Israelites made their way through the wilderness, both Aaron and Miriam began to question Moses' role as leader of all the people. *"Has the LORD indeed spoken only through Moses? Has he not spoken through us also? And the LORD heard it"* (Numbers 12:2). Upon hearing this, God called Moses, Aaron, and Miriam to meet with him in the tent of meeting. There, he explained why Moses' leadership was unique, unlike theirs. Then, he asked Aaron and Miriam a question that likely terrified them: *"Why then were you not afraid to speak against my servant Moses?"* (Numbers 12:8). There was no answer to this. Miriam was punished for this rebellion by becoming leprous (perhaps hers was the strongest voice advocating it), but Moses prayed for her. He and all the people loved her, and God restored her after seven days, for God loved her, too. Miriam had *received* wonderful gifts of leadership and prophecy from God, but she stumbled when she *grasped* for more. We are reminded of the other feminine acts of grasping we have seen in Eve and Sarah. They also turned out badly; surely there is a lesson here for us.

Miriam's stumble helps us see the dangers of jealousy, resentment, judging, and murmuring against God's appointed authority. Those make us fertile ground for the pride that can poison our souls. However, Miriam's bad moment was simply one bad moment, something that can happen to any of us. She was punished; she was healed and restored. Such is the kindness of God. Her reputation as a helper to Moses and Aaron remained untarnished. How do we know this? In the New Testament, we discover that many Jewish women bore her name; there "Miriam" is translated as "Mary." Their parents were happy to identify their daughters with one of Israel's great women of faith. We know from tradition that one humble, elderly couple, Joachim and Anne, chose that name for their precious daughter—Mary, who would one day become Israel's new Miriam.

Miriam and Mary

Miriam and Mary shared a name—was that just a coincidence? Or did one bear witness to the other?

We have seen that one distinguishing characteristic of Miriam's life was her courage, evident in the very first scene recorded in her story. When she hid in the reeds at the Nile and then rose up to expose herself, she must have known she was risking great danger, not just to herself but to her family as well. That exposure took courage. She was brave because she focused entirely on the child's life, not her own.

When God sent Miriam to help Moses and Aaron deliver his people, once again courage was required of her. This Pharaoh's wrath against the Hebrews was just as fierce as that of his predecessor who commanded the death of all Hebrew baby boys. After Pharoah stubbornly resisted Moses' constant command to let the people go, God sent an angel of death throughout Egypt that took the lives of all firstborn people and animals, beginning in the Pharaoh's own family. That finally convinced him; he expelled the Israelites from Egypt. It did not take long, however, for him to decide he had made a mistake. He and his armies took off after the Israelites, chasing them as far as the Red Sea. God told Moses to hold the people there at its shore, not to move from there. That left the Israelites with no place to hide except in its waters. It was a terrifying strategy, and it filled the people with *"great fear. And the sons of Israel cried out to the* LORD; *and they said to Moses, 'Is it because there are no graves in Egypt that you have taken us away to die in the wilderness ... it would have been better for us to serve the Egyptians than to die in the wilderness'"* (Exodus 14:10–12). Escape from certain slaughter looked impossible to them, and it was, humanly speaking, until God intervened in a miraculous way. The waters that the pursuing Egyptians thought would seal the former slaves' fate opened to secure their future as free people. Then, the waters closed over Pharaoh and his army; the enemy was completely vanquished.

We can imagine that when Miriam looked at the Israelites' impossible position on the shore of the Red Sea, she also felt the fear of inevitable doom. Rushing to Moses' side and begging him to change course must have seemed very inviting. To stand still and wait on God took enormous courage. To face down certain death always does. Though Scripture does not tell us, we can imagine that God's appointed leaders—Moses, Aaron, and Miriam—did not falter. It seems that they all showed magnificent courage, the kind that comes from great faith in the One who had called them. They knew that if God willed the terrifying plan that led them there, they had to obey him. By her obedience, Miriam became the first woman in Scripture to face down death out of allegiance to God, an example many others would follow, including Mary, her namesake.

When Gabriel announced a coming pregnancy to Mary, she also faced danger in obeying God's will. To be found pregnant *before* she had lived with Joseph, her betrothed, would be very hard to explain to him and to others. The charge of adultery, with its death sentence, could be leveled against her. At the very minimum, her reputation was at stake. Whispers and rumors could follow her wherever she went, for a very long time. It took courage for Mary to say yes to God's plan. Her willingness to give birth to this child, who would be the messianic Savior for whom her people had long waited, was much more important than all the risks she took. As Miriam had done at the Nile, Mary focused on the life of the child, not her own life. For both Miriam and Mary, God turned their willingness to sacrifice themselves into miraculous deliverance for them and their people.

When Mary and Joseph took the infant, Jesus, to present him at the Temple in obedience to the rites of Jewish law, Mary heard a prophecy about her son that had to strike some fear into her heart. Simeon, a devout and righteous Spirit-filled man, warned that Jesus would grow up to be *a sign that is spoken against,"* and he told Mary, *"A sword will pierce you own soul also"* (Luke 2:34–35). What mother, upon hearing these words, could escape their meaning? Did it take courage for Mary not to melt into the floor in anguish, beseeching God to change his plan, to prevent this kind of painful future for Jesus and herself? Like Miriam, Mary stood still and faithful to God's plan. There were many times in Mary's life when she needed to show the same courage that characterized Miriam's life. Sometimes courage can be thought of as primarily a masculine virtue, and it is certainly that. The stories of courageous Old Testament women show us something of *feminine* courage; Miriam gives us our first example.

Miriam also gives us other hints of the woman to come who would bear her name. Both Miriam and Mary had to protect the life of a child under a king's death sentence. Miriam's brother found safety in an Egyptian court. Mary's child could only find safety in a flight from home into Egypt. Miriam helped deliver God's people from their bondage to slavery. Mary helped deliver God's people from their bondage to sin and death. It was Miriam who was the first woman to sing out, for others to hear, great praise for God's mighty victory over an enemy. St. Ambrose saw Miriam as a type of the Church when she led God's redeemed people in songs of divine praise.[16] She began a long tradition that continues through the entire Old Testament. Mary, who was formed in this tradition of feminine songs of God's glory, continued it as she sang God's praises to Elizabeth, her Spirit-filled cousin, after conceiving the son who would defeat God's enemy, the Devil. We, God's redeemed people, are still singing her *Magnificat* today. We can see it was no coincidence that Mary bore Miriam's name.

— Pondering Miriam —

Miriam was a woman of firsts—the first woman to be named a leader and prophetess in Israel, the first woman we encounter in Scripture to sing a prayer song praising God's might. Yet she served as a helper to Moses and Aaron. When she grasped at more authority, outside the boundaries of her vocation, she was punished. A woman as interesting as Miriam surely has lessons for us. Here are some questions to help us ponder her life.

Not many of us will ever find ourselves risking certain death to obey God. If we do, Miriam gives us an example of how to do it. She stood *still and silent*, which is exactly what God wanted of his people at the Red Sea. Probably *all* of us, at one time or another, will need to practice courage, or fortitude, in this way. Courage enables us to face and resist danger, to see what must be done and do it without shrinking away in fear. It also enables us to endure pain, either physical, mental, or emotional; it is for the suffering that can come to us as we wait on God. Mary also had times in her life when she needed courage. Any of us who face times of choosing God's will over our own, who must undergo the "little deaths" to self, will need both aspects of this virtue.

- Is now one of those times for you? Can you find help in the examples of Miriam and Mary, who both showed great courage, confident they could trust God no matter what? Can you trust him with your life, as they did?

What a jubilant scene it must have been at the Red Sea when the Israelites, convinced God had truly freed them from their enemies, broke out into singing, dancing, and music making to express their gratitude to God, praising his glorious might. The image of Miriam leading the women in song is a lasting one, isn't it? The singing was likely antiphonal, with Moses and the men singing the stanzas, and Miriam with the women singing the refrain. Back and forth it went, a beautiful sound of the complementarity of male and female, just as God designed them. Both had voices, yet the voices were different; both praised God, but their sounds were unique.

We will encounter many singing women in the Old Testament. Here Miriam lifted her prayer song after she and God's people experienced deliverance from a profound threat of danger—either death or a return to slavery, which would have felt like death. Voices filled the desert air, glorifying God. Can there be any better way to use our voices than this?

- How are you using your voice today? Miriam gives us two examples to think about. Her voice led women in recognizing God's goodness to them and giving expression to that gratitude, but hers was also the voice of judgment, complaining, and perhaps jealousy—of questioning God's authority in Moses. We each have a choice, every day, of how best to use our feminine voices—in our families, at work, in public places, with our friends or with strangers, or in prayer. Can thinking carefully about this now help you to choose wisely today?

Miriam, for all her greatness, was called to be a *helper*. Although she was unmarried, without children, she lived a fruitful life in that role. When she grasped at more, she stepped outside of God's call to her. It did not go well. To be a helper requires humility, a willing acceptance of whatever smallness our role brings. Mary is, of course, our purest example of this kind of humility. As a Carmelite nun wrote,

> In her *Magnificat*, which has reverberated through the centuries, she sang, "*My soul proclaims the greatness of the Lord; my spirit rejoices in God my Savior. For he has looked with favor on his lowly servant.*" This canticle of her Immaculate Heart, luminous and perfectly humble in its recognition that *she was both a radically dependent creature and a beloved daughter*, seized God with delight and he raised her above angels and saints as their Queen.[17]

Do you struggle in your feminine vocation as helper? Does impatience or frustration with the leadership of others tempt you to grasp it for yourself? Does the smallness of your life—perhaps housebound with children, sickness, or age—tempt you to think your life is unimportant? Do you resent being passed over for promotion at work or feel jealous of the success or notoriety of others? If so, can the fruitfulness of both Miriam and Mary, who lived their vocations as helpers to the full, give you encouragement today?

- Are there any lingering impressions from Miriam's life that you do not want to forget? Perhaps you can write them down here or in your own journal.

Chapter Four

Rahab—In the Time of the Conquest and Judges, Part I

"And she said, 'According to your words, so be it.'"

–Joshua 2:21

> *Historical Context: Conquest and Judges (1406–1050 BC)*

After Moses died during the desert wanderings, the Israelites finally entered the Promised Land under the leadership of Joshua. When the people arrived again at Canaan in about 1406 BC, at the beginning of the era of the Conquest and Judges, Joshua sent two men in to spy out the land. They were to give special attention to Jericho, a fortified city on the border. It is there that we meet Rahab.

The Woman, Rahab

Rahab is the first person we meet living in the land of Canaan. While the Israelites lived in Egypt, the Canaanites had moved in and taken over the land God gave to Abraham as their home. They practiced idolatry, and theirs was a culture of pagan immorality. Rahab worked as a prostitute, or harlot, in the city of Jericho; she was owner of an "inn" where men came and went. The two Israelite spies sent by Joshua to do reconnaissance in the city went there first, thinking Rahab's inn would be an easy place to blend in and not be discovered. They were wrong.

A report of their presence in the inn aroused the king's suspicion, so he sent men to Rahab with these words: *"Bring forth the men that have come to you, who entered your house; for they have come to search out all the land"* (Joshua 2:3). However, Rahab had hidden the spies on her roof, so she sent the king's men off on a wild goose chase, telling them, *"True, men came to me, but I did not know where they came from; and when the gate was to be closed, at dark, the men went out; where the men went I do not know; pursue them quickly, for you will overtake them"* (Joshua 2:4–5). The king's men left her and headed toward the Jordan River, and when they had left, the city gate closed behind them.

If we stopped the action of the story here, we might think that although Rahab did know the men were Israelite spies (why else would she hide them?), to her they were simply two more paying customers whom she did not want to lose. She might have needed the money; business might have been more important to her than helping the king track down his enemies. However, before the spies lay down for the night, Rahab went up on the roof to talk to them, and that is when we discover this episode was far more than business as usual. She said, *"I know that the Lord has given you the land, and that fear of you has fallen upon us, and that all the inhabitants of the land melt away before you"* (Joshua 2:9). She went on to tell them how the Canaanites knew all about how miraculously and powerfully God delivered the Israelites from bondage in Egypt, as well as the victories against enemies he had given them during their desert wanderings. Then she said, *"As soon as we heard it, our hearts melted, and there was no courage left in any man, because of you"* (Joshua 2:11).

How different Rahab's report of the land of Canaan was from the report of the spies Moses had sent a generation earlier. Rather than seeing that the Canaanites feared the approaching Israelites, this had been their report: *"The land ... is a land that devours its inhabitants; and all the people that we saw in it are men of great stature ... and we seemed to ourselves like grasshoppers, and so we seemed to them"* (Numbers 13:32–33). Naturally, this report did not stir up enthusiasm in the people who heard it to proceed with the attack. They rose in rebellion and refused to go in to take the land God wanted to give them. As Jeff Cavins and Tim Gray explain, though, here is what the spies had missed:

> However strong [the Canaanites] were in numbers, arms, and fortifications, [they] had lost all courage because they had heard what God had done for Israel ... God's miraculous deeds had set Israel up for taking the land without much of a fight ... What Israel could have won with simple obedience will now have to be taken by force."[18]

The Canaanites' fear and dread of the Israelites had too much time to harden into stubborn resistance and determined refusal to let them set foot in the land God had promised them. For Rahab, however, the news about what God had done for his people produced a very different response. She acknowledged, *"The Lᴏʀᴅ your God is he who is God in heaven above and on earth beneath"* (Joshua 2:11). If only Pharaoh, years earlier, had been able to know the meaning of all the signs and wonders God worked before his own eyes through Moses. Rahab did know:

Her opening words, '*I know*,' hearken back to Pharaoh, who
refused to 'know' Yahweh, and to the plagues sent so that
Egypt and its king would 'know' that Yahweh is the one true
God. Rahab, a Canaanite harlot, confesses to both *know* and
believe the lesson of the Exodus that Yahweh is '*God in heaven
above and on earth beneath*.'"[19]

This woman had undergone a conversion so profound and
complete that she was willing to risk her life and face death as a
traitor to help the Israelites retake the land God clearly wanted
to give them. Hers was the first recorded Gentile conversion
to faith in the God of Abraham, Isaac, and Jacob recorded in
Scripture, a conversion that would be remembered and revered
throughout all the ages, even to our own.

After confessing her faith in their God, Rahab asked the
spies to deal kindly with her and her extended family, "*to deliver
our lives from death*" (Joshua 2:13) during the battle soon to
come. The spies gave her a beautiful response, full of meaning:
"*Our life for yours!*" (Joshua 2:14). They sealed themselves into a
commitment to her with covenantal language. Think how often
God spoke to his people in this kind of language: "*You shall be my
people, and I will be your God*" (Jeremiah 30:22), or "You are mine,
I am yours"—an exchange of lives. The spies recognized Rahab's
devotion in heart and mind to the God they served. She had, at
that moment, become one with them and all Israel; they made a
nuptial vow to her.

Then Rahab lowered the spies down on a rope through a
window and gave them instructions about where to hide and
for how long. As they left, they gave her a sign guaranteeing
her family's protection when the attack began. That was a wise

thought; Rahab may have wondered how the Israelites would know her family needed to be spared, considering the chaos in which battles were fought. She was to hang a scarlet cord from the window. All her family were to be gathered in the house. If anyone left the house or told others about what would soon happen, protection would be lost. This is reminiscent of how the Israelites had to paint their doors with blood in order to be spared when the angel of death went through Egypt taking the lives of the firstborn. Anyone leaving the house left behind the blood's protection. Both these episodes point forward to the salvific blood of Jesus, the Lamb of God, which spares sinners from death.

When Rahab heard all the details of the plan to save her and her family—of what she had to believe and to do—she said, "*According to your words, so be it*" (Joshua 2:21). She was ready to do all that was required of her for the deliverance of her family. The risk to her was not over. A red cord hanging from her window could easily be seen by others and just as easily arouse suspicion about her again. Rahab would have known that, yet she humbly submitted to the spies' instructions and did exactly what they said.

During the great battle of Jericho, Rahab and all her family were saved. She lived as a permanent resident in Israel (see Joshua 6:25). In St. Matthew's genealogy of Jesus, she is listed as the wife of Salmon and the mother of Boaz, ancestor of David, the king (Matthew 1:5). Rahab's profession of faith and her willingness to act on it would "graft her into the very bloodlines of Abrahamic blessing that brings salvation to the world."[20] The early Church held Rahab in great esteem for two reasons. First, her remarkable conversion from the life of a prostitute to life as a devout follower of the God of Israel and her inclusion in the genealogy of Jesus make her a stellar example of God's rich mercy to sinners. Additionally, Rahab was often mentioned by the Fathers as a type of the Church:

> This Rahab, although she is called a prostitute, nevertheless is a sign of the virgin Church, considered as a foreshadow of the coming realities at the end of the age ... Just as the apostle says, *'An unfaithful wife is sanctified through her faithful husband'* (1 Cor 7:14), so also is the Church, coming from the infidelity of the Gentiles and prostitution with idols, sanctified through the body of Christ, of which we are members ... therefore the Church is found in the figure of Rahab, the hostess of saints.[21]

Rahab, with great faith and humility, was a helper to the Israelite spies. Both Jewish and Christian history have never forgotten her.

Rahab and Mary

A prostitute who owned a brothel as a type of Mary, the pure Virgin Mother of God—preposterous! So it seems at first thought. Yet now that we know more of Rahab's story, we can reach a very different conclusion.

First, we will need to go back to Eden to hear the promise God made to Adam and Eve after the Fall: *"I will put enmity between you and the woman, between your seed and her seed; he shall bruise your head, and you shall bruise his heel"* (Genesis 3:15). God's response to the Serpent's evil in the Garden was to send another man and woman—a mother and son—to defeat him. We are told little about either one at this point in our story, but two things are clear. They will be entirely on God's side, and they will be warriors in his definitive battle to defeat his enemy. If we are looking in the Old Testament for types—men and women who foreshadow this mother and son—we should expect to see some of those types engaged in battles.

Rahab is the first feminine type of warrior whom we encounter in Scripture. Recall that Miriam, another type of Mary, was not herself part of any battle raging around her. The Israelites miraculously escaped that kind of battle with the pursuing Egyptians; Miriam sang about God's triumph against them. In Rahab, we meet a woman in the thick of an attack. She deserves our attention as a possible type of the mother-warrior who was to come.

As soon as we begin to think about Rahab's life, we start to see the hints of Mary she gives us. First, based upon her whole-hearted belief in the God of Israel, she was willing to risk death, accused as a traitor, so God's people could enter Canaan, the Promised Land, and live free and in peace. At the Annunciation, upon hearing what God wanted her to do, Mary was willing to risk death, accused as an adulteress, so his people could enter their homeland of heaven to live free and in peace forever.

Then, when Rahab heard the details of what she needed to *believe* and to *do* to save herself and her family from death, she humbly answered in these simple words: *"According to your words, so be it"* (Joshua 2:21). When Mary heard the details of what she needed both to believe and to do to save God's family, she humbly answered in these simple words: *"Let it be to me according to your word"* (Luke 1:38).

Finally, both Rahab and Mary served in pivotal battles that God's people waged against their enemies—Rahab in an earthly battle and Mary in a spiritual one—as helpers armed with faith.

Joshua, not Rahab, led the battle of Jericho. Jesus, not Mary, led the battle against the Devil. Both women played dramatic, heroic roles as helpers to victory. About Rahab, the New Testament says: *"By faith, Rahab the harlot did not perish with those who were disobedient, because she had given friendly welcome to the spies"* (Hebrews 11:31). Her *"friendly welcome to the spies"* was the only weapon she used in the battle, a weapon that came from her faith. About Mary, her cousin, Elizabeth said, *"Blessed is she who believed that there would be a fulfillment of what was spoken to her from the Lord"* (Luke 1:45). Faith was Mary's weapon, too. Both women became mothers of the household of faith; both have places in the genealogy of our Savior, Jesus Christ; both are types of the Church, his Bride.

God used their smallness to make them great.

— *Pondering Rahab* —

The first thing we learned about Rahab in her story was that she was a harlot, keeper of a brothel. Her conversion away from that life to become a mother in the household of faith captivated the Early Church Fathers, as St. Cyril of Jerusalem shows us:

> But perhaps even among women someone will say, I have committed fornication, and adultery. I have defiled my body by excesses of all kinds: is there salvation for me? *Turn thine eyes, O woman, upon Rahab, and look thou also for salvation*; for if she who had been openly and publicly a harlot was saved by repentance, is not she who on some occasion before receiving grace committed fornication to be saved by repentance and fasting?[22]

All of us need to be reminded by dramatic examples like Rahab's that God has mercy on sinners. In the New Testament, we know, Jesus had a remarkable conversation with the Samaritan woman at the well (see John 4:1–30). She, too, had a troubled relationship with men, yet she became an energetic witness to the Messiah, revered even today as St. Photina.

- Is Rahab's story speaking to you in this way today? Sexual failures from our past can sometimes rise to crush our spirits and paralyze us. They can fill us with regret and shame. We can see from Rahab's story that if we know who God is and act on what we know of how he wants us to live, there is more than enough of his mercy to cleanse and restore us with his promise of mercy. The Sacrament of Reconciliation can renew our relationship with God no matter what is in our past.

Both Rahab and Mary risked their lives to do God's will in battles they faced. We, too, can find ourselves in a battle whenever we must take a risk in following God's will that is revealed to us in the teachings of the Church. Ours is an internal battle; we can feel it fiercely in ourselves. For example: Do I risk getting pregnant if I follow the Church's teaching on artificial contraception? Do I risk having to remain in a difficult marriage if I follow the Church's teaching on divorce? Do I risk straining my finances if I follow the Church's teaching on tithing?

- Are you experiencing an internal battle like this today? Do you know what God wants but struggle with what it might cost you? Can you ask for God's grace and the prayers of Mother Mary to be able to say to him like Rahab: "*According to your words, so be it*"? (Joshua 2:21)

There is an appealing beauty in the way the epistle to the Hebrews describes Rahab's faith: "*She had given friendly welcome to the spies*" (Hebrews 11:31). This seems so simple! Of course, her "*friendly welcome*" included risking her own safety. For us, small acts of love done for love of God or others, although not risking our lives, can cost us inconvenience, discomfort, being misunderstood, or perhaps just the sting of not getting our own way. It is part of Rahab's glory that she is remembered for this "*friendly welcome*" in what is often called the "Heroes of Faith Hall of Fame" in Hebrews 11.

- Do you sometimes think your life is too small to make a difference in God's kingdom? Can you, instead, think about what small, simple things you can do today for love of God or others that can grow your faith? Greatness is not our goal, faith is. We must remember that God *delights* in making smallness great (see CCC **489**).

Are there any lingering impressions from Rahab's life that you do not want to forget? Perhaps you can write them down here or in your own journal.

....

....

....

....

....

....

....

....

....

Chapter Five

Deborah and Jael—
In the Time of the Conquest
and Judges, Part II

"You arose, Deborah, arose as a mother in Israel."

–Judges 5:7

"Most blessed of women be Jael ... of tent-dwelling
women most blessed."

–Judges 5:24

Historical Context: Conquest and Judges (1406–1050 BC)

After Joshua and the Israelites conquered Jericho, it took the people many years to reclaim the Promised Land from the Canaanites. These years of the Conquest and Judges time period were tumultuous, ending in about 1050 BC. Joshua's leadership was strong and faithful to all that Moses commanded him to do as his successor. After his death, however, the people struggled to remain faithful to their covenant with God. They regularly fell into the idolatry practiced by the Canaanites in that land. A cycle developed during this time consisting of covenant infidelity, God's punishment—they were overcome by their enemies—their cry for his help, his provision of a leader or "judge" to deliver them, and peace for several years. Then, it began all over again. During this period, the judges called by God to lead the people were at first good and faithful, but they gradually descended to being weak and sometimes disreputable people toward its end. Still, even with all its decline and disorder, in the period of the Conquest and Judges we meet two remarkable women, Deborah and Jael. They were bright lights in what would soon become a time of descending darkness in Israel.

The Women, Deborah and Jael

Deborah was a uniquely gifted woman who offered guidance and correction to Israel during her time as its fourth judge. She was married to a man named Lappidoth, but Scripture does not mention any children born to them. Yet, paradoxically, Deborah is remembered as *"a mother in Israel,"* as we shall soon see. In her civil role as judge, she sat *"under the palm of Deborah ... in the hill country of Ephraim; and the sons of Israel came up to her for judgment"* (Judges 4:5). Considering what a turbulent, chaotic time this was in Israel, this shaded, peaceful scene where *"the sons of Israel"* could find help for their problems from a wise woman is refreshing.

Deborah was also a prophetess (see Judges 4:4), the second woman in salvation history, after Miriam, to have this role. In her work as a judge, she could dispense justice in contentious grievances, as well as provide divine direction for the Israelites to live as God's people. She did not perform military or liturgical service. As judge and prophetess, she was able to fully exercise the remarkable gifts God gave her within her feminine vocation.

One day God told her to summon Barak, the commander

of Israel's ragtag army, with this message: *"Go, gather your men at Mount Tabor ... And I will draw Sisera, the general of* [the Canaanites'] *army ... with his chariots and his troops; and I will give him into your hand"* (Judges 4:6–7). These words make very clear that God intended the Israelites to enter a battle that would have a victorious outcome; God himself would fight on their side to guarantee it. Nevertheless, Barak balked. He said to Deborah: *"If you will go with me, I will go; but if you will not go with me, I will not go"* (Judges 4:8). What was he thinking?

Barak was likely weighing up the lopsided effort a battle like that would surely be. The Canaanite army was large, well trained, and fully equipped. The much smaller Israelite army would fight with untrained volunteers and makeshift weapons. The odds against victory were enormous. Barak must have thought that Deborah, because of her wisdom and prophetic gift, would be the source of the certain victory God had promised. Without her presence in the battle, he refused to go. Because his vocation was to be a military commander, this was grave disobedience. Deborah recognized it right away: *"I will surely go with you; nevertheless, the road on which you are going will not lead to your glory, for the LORD will sell Sisera into the hand of a woman"* (Judges 4:9). Deborah understood what Barak completely missed. This battle belonged to God, and he would give the victory, not Deborah. Barak's punishment would be a humiliation to him. His enemy would be defeated by *"the hand of a woman."* No soldier wanted to be remembered that way.

To his credit, Barak did rally the Israelite forces: *"ten thousand men went up at his heels; and Deborah went up with them"* (Judges 4:10). In this battle, Deborah never took up arms. The only reason she was there at all was Barak's failure to live his vocation. She served as his helper, and the help she gave was most powerful. In her strong, confident voice she called out to Barak: *"Up! For this is the day in which the LORD has given Sisera into your hand. Does not the LORD go out before you?"* (Judges 4:14). With this encouragement, Barak was able to lead his outnumbered army to victory over the Canaanites, just as God had promised through Deborah, his prophetess. Sisera, however, decided to escape when he saw he had been defeated. He fled to what he thought would be safety, the tent of a woman named Jael. She was married to a Kenite, a member of a Gentile clan related to Moses through marriage. They were often allied with Israel in conquering the Promised Land. The Kenites and Canaanites were not at war with each other at that time, so Jael's tent seemed like a safe refuge to Sisera. That was the last mistake he ever made.

Jael welcomed Sisera into her tent, giving him milk to quench his thirst and covering him with a blanket as he lay down to rest his weary body after the brutal battle. Before falling asleep, he called out to her to stand watch at the tent's door to prevent an enemy finding him. She must have suspected right away that he had escaped a battle with the Israelites; his commander's attire and fear of being found gave him away. She likely feared that more trouble was on the way to her tent, putting her in great danger. Perhaps her sympathies lay with the Israelites. She wanted to help them prevail against this cowardly enemy. So, Jael did as he requested until he succumbed to his desperate need for sleep. Then, she *"took a tent peg, and took a hammer in her hand, and went softly to him and drove the peg into his temple, till it went down into the ground ... So he died"* (Judges 4:21). The Kenites were not at war with the Canaanites, but neither were they at war with the Israelites who, in this woman's tent, had a courageous friend.

In Deborah and Jael, we meet women who were warriors. We recall that Rahab was a woman around whom a battle raged, yet she remained safe in her house. These two women had more active roles in the battle to free the Israelites from tyrannous Canaanite rule. Deborah, the judge and prophetess, aroused, directed, and then encouraged the Israelite army. She did not herself engage in combat. Jael did not go out with an army, either. She was simply tending to her tent in her feminine vocation as wife. When the enemy showed up at her door, she knew what she had to do. Without any knowledge of Deborah's prophetic word to Barak—*"the Lord will sell Sisera into the hand of a woman"*—she stepped into the role of victor God had ordained. Without their leader, the Canaanite army was thoroughly vanquished, and there was peace and freedom in Israel: *"the land had rest for forty years"* (Judges 5:31).

After the battle, both Barak and Deborah sang a prayer song that included details of how God won their fight against a much greater military strength (see Judges 5). We have long known this as Deborah's Song, because without ever taking up arms, she guided the battle to victory. It was sung in the third person, addressing both Deborah and Barak (see Judges 5:12) in a way that preserves humility. The song begins with a surprise. Considering that it goes on to describe a mighty and miraculous battle, it begins with blessing the Lord that *"the leaders took the lead in Israel, that the people offered themselves willingly to fight their enemy"* (Judges 5:2). Instead of the boasting in which victors who have overcome great odds often indulge, Deborah first blessed the Lord and then cherished the volunteer soldiers who heeded God's call to trust him for the victory. Here is distinctly feminine leadership, exercised in humility and a tenderness for the people engaged in the battle, not just its outcome. This is evidence of why *"the sons of Israel"* traveled to the shade of that palm under which Deborah dispensed justice. She was a wise woman who acknowledged God's greatness and was also able to see what was good and noble in people, not dwelling on what was weak and cowardly. We remember how Barak balked at first when God commanded him to lead the fight. In the prayer song, Deborah acknowledged the failures of those who stayed home from the battle (see Judges 5:15–17) without insult or condemnation.

The prayer song goes on to describe how beaten down and disorganized Israel was at that time in its history. In those days *"caravans ceased and travelers kept to the byways. The peasantry ceased in Israel, they ceased until you arose, Deborah, arose as a mother in Israel"* (Judges 5:6–7). Deborah was called *"a mother"* because she did for the nation what mothers do for their children: listened to their complaints against each other and dispensed wise justice, taught them what God wanted them to do and encouraged them to do it, saw with tenderness what was good in them and worthy of praise, and was always an example of one who had complete trust in God's goodness and care for them. She went into battle when they were threatened, yet humbly remained within her feminine vocation of helper. Without biological children, she beautifully fulfilled her vocation as mother to God's family.

Deborah's song gives us glimpses of what a godly mother-warrior looks like. In it, she blessed the Lord in its very first words, as well as lauding the courage and faith of those who gave themselves willingly to do as he commanded. She delighted in Jael's exalted position of *"most blessed of women."* She had sympathy for the pain any mother would have over her son's delayed homecoming after battle—even the mother of an enemy (see Judges 5:28). Deborah's story gives us wonderful hints of the mother-warrior God promised in Eden as the whole world waited for her appearance.

Deborah, Jael, and Mary

Deborah appeared during Israel's history as a mother-warrior who fought victoriously against the nation's enemy, all without any weapons other than faith, courage, obedience, and love for her people. She foreshadowed Mary, the mother-warrior for whom creation waited. As St. John Paul II has written about God's response to the Fall,

> The Lord says to the serpent, the personification of evil: '*I will put enmity between you and the woman, between your seed and her seed...*' According to the sacred author's narrative, the Lord's first reaction to sin is not to punish the guilty but to offer them the hope of salvation and to involve them actively in the work of redemption, showing his great generosity even to those who have offended him. [These words] also reveal the unique destiny of the woman who, although yielding to the temptation before the man did, in virtue of the divine plan later became God's first ally. Overturning this situation, God declares that he will make the woman the serpent's enemy."[23]

If we look for a battle anywhere in Nazareth on the day Gabriel visited Mary, we will look in vain. However, if we look at the vision of heaven given to St. John in the book of Revelation, we will find warfare:

> "*A great sign appeared in heaven, a woman clothed with the sun, with the moon under her feet, and on her head a crown of twelve*

stars; she was with child ... And another sign appeared ... a great red dragon ... And the dragon stood before the woman who was about to bear a child, that he might devour her child when she brought it forth ... a male child, one who is to rule all the nations ... but her child was caught up to God and to his throne, and the woman fled into the wilderness, where she has a place prepared by God in which to be nourished" (Revelation 12:1–6).

St. John gives us the apocalyptic version of what took place when Mary gave her *fiat* to God and bore his Son. In the quiet of that little village of Nazareth, the battle had begun. Mary's weapons in this battle were her faith, courage, obedience, and love for God's people. Unlike Deborah, she did not go up with Israel's army to a hilltop and shout directions and encouragement to the troops. Mary, in the thick of the great and final battle, whispered words that would herald its start, like the sound of a celestial trumpet blast: *"Let it be to me according to your word"* (Luke 1:38). For both Deborah and Mary, victory was certain.

In Deborah's time, Israel's covenant fidelity was spotty and weak. It took God's correction of letting their enemies overcome them to wake them up. When the dissolution of the people's solidarity under God's rule seemed nearly complete, Deborah arose as *"a mother in Israel,"* helping them return to the loving care God wanted to give them. She gave wisdom to those seeking it, direction to those needing it, and encouragement to keep them all strong and motivated. In Mary's quiet, humble earthly life, she was mother first to her son, Jesus. He spent thirty years with her. Hers was the first human face his infant eyes saw, the first human body to nourish him, the first human heart to love him unconditionally. In the long life Jesus shared with his mother, she did all the things good mothers do. She may not have known it then, in the early years, but she was just beginning her vocation as mother of the New Israel, the Church, those who, as St. John tells us in his vision, *"keep the commandments of God and bear testimony to Jesus"* (Revelation 12:17). Deborah generously acknowledged Jael's blessedness for slaying their enemy. She had no resentment of sharing the glory of their victory with her. Mary once stood at the door of a house, looking for Jesus. When told of her presence there, Jesus said to those listening, *"'Who is my mother, and who are my brethren?' And stretching out his hand toward his disciples, he said, 'Here are my mother and my brethren! For whoever does the will of my Father in heaven is my brother, and sister, and mother'"* (Matthew 12:48–50). Mary did not resent sharing her maternity with his disciples. As John Paul II wrote in *Redemptoris Mater*, "The new spiritual motherhood of which Jesus spoke is primarily concerned with [Mary]. Is not Mary the first of those who 'hear the word of God and do it?'"[24]

As Jesus was dying on the Cross, he knew the best gift he could give his followers was the gift of his mother as their own. In Deborah's time, troubled Israel needed a strong, godly mother to care for the nation. Jesus knew that in the world his people, the Church, would likewise need a strong, godly mother's care. From that moment at the foot of the Cross, Mother Mary has been exactly that.

Deborah had a decisive role in a hard-won battle against impossible odds. After the victory, she sang a prayer song that revealed her trust in God's character, his faithfulness, his care for his people. Mary also had a decisive role in a hard-won battle against impossible odds. The prayer song she sang, the *Magnificat*, reveals her trust in God's character, his faithfulness, his care for his people, too.

Then, there is Jael. In a way, she can almost seem incidental to this dramatic story that finds its conclusion in her tent. Perhaps surprisingly, the Fathers of the Church did not think of her that way at all. For example, see what Origen at the turn of the third century wrote about her:

> "The woman, Jael, that foreigner about whom Deborah's prophecy said that victory would be *'through the hand of a woman'* (Jud 4:9), symbolizes the Church, which was assembled from foreign nations ... She killed him with a stake, then, which is to say that she overthrew him by the power and cunning of the wood of the cross."[25]

Origen saw Jael as a type of the Church, which has through the ages constantly battled her enemy, Satan, by means of the victory Jesus won on the wood of his Cross. Additionally, Jael is the first woman in salvation history about whom it was said that she was *"most blessed of women"* (Judges 5:24). What made her blessed was that she drove that tent peg into the enemy's head, finishing him off with one shattering pound of her hammer. This episode first takes us back to Eden, to God's promise of a battle in which the serpent receives a head wound—fatal for a serpent. The *"woman"* in that promise gives birth to the *"seed"* who delivers the mortal blow. The "woman" and her "seed" would *both* participate in his defeat, just as in the Garden Adam and Eve both participated in the serpent's victory over them. Then, the blessing on Jael takes us forward to Mary, when her cousin, Elizabeth, also hailed her as *"blessed among women,"* (Luke 1:42) because *"she believed that there would be a fulfillment of what was spoken to her from the LORD"* (Luke 1:45). Mary's faith enabled her *fiat* to God's will for her.

She gave her body so that God could take flesh within her womb. Years earlier, when Mary and Joseph presented the infant Jesus at the Temple, Simeon saw a vision of this moment when he held the boy in his arms, blessed God, and told Mary that *"a sword will pierce through your own soul also"* (Luke 2:35). In this, he described how the soldier's lance that struck Jesus in his side to make sure he was dead (see John 19:34) would, at the same time, pierce Mary's soul. It was not simply that Mary would experience horrific pain in watching her son die, which she certainly did. It was that in her participation in God's great battle against his enemy, her own flesh and blood would be pierced as Jesus was nailed to the tree. As Fr. Reginald Garrigou-Lagrange, OP, the great French Dominican theologian, has written: "Tradition is clear on Mary's union with the Redeemer; it never tires of repeating that as Eve was united to the first man in the work of perdition Mary was united to the Redeemer in the work of redemption."[26] Of course, the Church has always taught that Jesus alone is our Redeemer; he redeemed Mary by preserving her from original sin. Her role was to be his helper in our redemption. Eve helped Adam sin; Mary helped Jesus save us from sin. As a medieval saying attributed to St. Albert the Great says, "The Blessed Virgin Mary was chosen by God not to be His minister but to be His consort and His helper—*in consortium et adjutorium*—according to the words of Genesis: Let us make him a help like to himself."[27]

Jael was a woman who was minding her tent far away from the noise, the blood, the mayhem of a raging battle. When the enemy sought her out, she quickly devised a plan for his defeat. While offering kind hospitality, she quietly, without a single recorded word in Scripture, drove wood into the enemy's head, fulfilling Deborah's prophetic word. She thus gives us Scripture's

first type of a woman—the mother-warrior promised in Eden—
who would someday do the same.

St. Ambrose, a Father of the Church in the fourth century,
saw in both Deborah and Jael types of the Church:

> So, then, Deborah foretold the event of the battle ... Jael
> carried off the triumph ... who in a mystery revealed to us
> the rising of the Church from the Gentiles. ... according to
> this history a woman ... became a judge, a woman set all in
> order, a woman prophesied, a woman triumphed, and joining
> in the battle array taught men to war under a woman's lead.
> But in a mystery, it is the battle of the faith and the victory of
> the Church.[28]

Mary, Mother of the Church, goes into battle with us, as well.

— Pondering Deborah —

Perhaps we might wonder if women who lived so long ago, whose stories we learn entirely within the context of a raging battle, would have anything to say to us. They could become just interesting characters in history or theology, of no practical help. We should not let that happen.

First, Deborah deserves our attention as the first feminine professional in Scripture. She had the job of civil judge at a time in Israel when a judge served as the one thin link the nation had to any kind of order and direction. Additionally, she had a prophetic gift from God. For a people whose covenant fidelity to the God who loved them was tenuous and uneven, she became God's voice to ears that had nearly gone completely deaf to him. As important as she was, her "office" was about ten miles outside of Jerusalem. She sat in the shade of a palm tree to do her work, in the quiet of a remote spot away from the bustle of the nearest town. Everything about that scene of her giving professional help to those who sought it—"*the sons of Israel*"—speaks of how feminine leadership works best. We imagine that she became an oasis of calm, of clear direction between right and wrong, always guided by God's voice of justice and love of goodness. She had a tenderness that saw beyond outcome to *people*, with a heart that looked for what was good or laudable in them. When she had to go into battle with Barak and the army, she remained within her feminine vocation. She directed and encouraged, but she did not take charge. When the victory was won, she sang a humble song of blessing to God for his faithfulness, for the soldiers who obeyed his call, and, in generosity of heart, for Jael, into whose hand he delivered the enemy.

All of us have vocations; for some of us, those are professional. What can Deborah's example teach us?

- Are you someone whose professional vocation takes you into contact with people needing your service? If so, are there ways you can make your workplace—from your home, office, building, in travel, etc.—a shaded place of rest? Can your tone of voice, your facial expression, your physical demeanor, and the words you use give clients or customers relief from the hothouse of professional life? Can people count on you as a person of clarity between right and wrong, between wise and foolish, between light and dark?
- Do you look for what is good and laudable in clients or coworkers, especially those who are difficult?
- If you experience great success in the project or job you have been given, is your first response to sing a silent blessing on God for his kindness to you?
- When coworkers or competitors win a victory you hoped would be yours, are you able to commend them for a job well done?
- When strong, firm leadership is required in your professional work, can you do it with the feminine humility of a *helper*, seeing yourself as assisting others with the gift of leadership God has given you?

We are separated from Deborah by centuries, but her lessons to us are fresh and relevant when we take time to ponder them. Are there any lingering impressions from Deborah's life that you do not want to forget? Perhaps you can write them down at the end of this chapter or in your own journal.

— *Pondering Jael* —

Jael, in a life very different from Deborah's, speaks to us from the quiet of her tent. Hers was a domestic vocation, with no apparent gifts or opportunities for leadership. Wouldn't we love to know more about her and what led her to kill Sisera when he sought refuge in her home? Perhaps the lack of details about this woman is a part of what make it necessary for us to listen more carefully to what she can tell us, because many of us live our lives as seemingly incidental to the big story of whatever is going on around us. We are not in the thick of things. We are not professionals. We are simply minding our homes, caring for husbands and children if we have them, daily doing the things that need doing. How can such simple lives be of any real consequence?

Jael tells us that great victories can be hidden in the appearance of simplicity. If we read her story in its spiritual sense, the enemy came into her tent and tried to make himself comfortable there. She had to resist him with what we can now see as a type of the Cross of Jesus—she drove wood into his head. With her action, she foreshadowed the greatest event in our human story—the definitive defeat of our enemy,

Satan. In this, she elicited for the first time in salvation history the accolade *"most blessed of women."* There was nothing simple about Jael's life.

- Are you someone whose vocation seems small because you are relatively housebound, without much opportunity for influence beyond the boundaries of the home? Reading Jael's story in its spiritual sense, can you see that the Enemy has his eye on just such a tent as yours? There is something vitally important to God's kingdom going on there that can catch his attention. Is it the creation and formation of children, the next generation in the Church's march through time? Is it the care for the elderly, the sick, or the disabled? Is it the kind hospitality you sometimes can offer visitors? Is it the loving encouragement of your phone calls or emails to family and friends who need it?

- Whatever the reason for your smallness, can you see that quiet, simple, ordinary homes like yours, in which God's faithful people live and carry on their daily lives, are outposts of light in his kingdom? They present a threat to Satan, the master of darkness. Jael defeated her enemy by the wood of a tent peg. Can you defeat him with the wood of the Cross when he appears at your door? How will he appear, we wonder. He sows seeds of doubt in us about God's love. He ignites fears of the future, our own or that of others. He stirs up divisions in families. He tempts us with the lure of material comforts. He feeds gossip about others into our ears and can start our tongues wagging in judgment of them. He whispers the dreaded question that chills and numbs our souls: "Is this all there is to my life?"

The victory over his lies, his darkness, his relentless rebellion against God is the victory of Christ's Cross. St. Paul, in his epistle to the Ephesians, tells us how to equip ourselves for the battle it takes to defeat our enemy, however he tries to gain a foothold in our homes:

> Therefore take the whole armor of God, that you may be able to withstand in the evil day, and having done all, to stand ... having fastened the belt of truth around your waist, and having put on the breastplate of righteousness, and having shod your feet with the equipment of the gospel of peace; besides all these, taking the shield of faith, with which you can quench all the flaming darts of the Evil One. And take the helmet of salvation, and the sword of the Spirit, which is the word of God." (Ephesians 6:13–17)

The victory of the wood of the Cross makes all these weapons available to us. Can you put them to good use when the Enemy knocks at your door?

- Are there any lingering impressions from Jael's life that you do not want to forget? Perhaps you can write them down here or in your own journal.

....

....

....

Chapter Six

Hannah—In the Time of the Conquest and Judges, Part III

"My heart exults in the LORD,
my strength is exalted in the LORD."

—1 Samuel 2:1

Historical Context: Conquest and Judges (1406–1050 BC)

Toward the end of the time of the Conquest and Judges, Israel was in such a state of disunity and disorder that it became necessary for the nation to ask God for a king to rule them. Of course, they already had a king—the Lord God himself—but they wanted a king they could see, as other nations had (see 1 Samuel 8). How would this transition happen? How would a king be anointed in a land that had never had one? In that moment, the man God chose to lead Israel in this turning point was born, Samuel. First, however, we meet his mother, Hannah, whose name means "grace" in Hebrew. Her story gives us a beautiful lesson in the meaning of that word.

The Woman, Hannah

Hannah was married to a devout man, Elkanah, who had two wives. Polygamy, a great departure from God's original design for marriage described in Genesis, was a concession to the weakness of human flesh the Fall brought with it. Elkanah probably married Hannah first but, when she proved to be barren, married a second wife, Peninnah, who was quite fertile (see 1 Samuel 1:2). Elkanah and his family went up every year from their home in Ramah to Shiloh, then the center of liturgical worship in Israel, *"to worship and sacrifice to the Lord"* (1 Samuel 1:3). When Elkanah offered cooked portions of their animal sacrifice to his family at their meal, he gave portions to Peninnah and all her children. *"Although he loved Hannah,"* he gave her only one portion, *"because the Lord had closed her womb"* (1 Samuel 1:5). Peninnah used to ridicule Hannah about her infertility, causing her great pain *"year by year"* (1 Samuel 1:7), in every visit to Shiloh. Hannah remained silent during this verbal assault, without retaliation. Yet this torment made her so upset that she lost her appetite, shedding tears instead of eating. Elkanah did not understand her reaction: *"Hannah, why do you weep and why do you not eat? And why is your heart sad? Am I not more to you than ten sons?"* (1 Samuel 1:8). He had deep affection for his wife; he did not hold her barrenness against her. His question pinpoints how a wife's pain of infertility can be mysterious to her husband. A wife can know her husband loves her, that he does not treat her as guilty for their lack of children. He can make his love for her as clear as he knows how to do, but he sees that his love does not fill the void she feels from an empty womb. This is a great suffering for both husband and wife.

One year, when the family was in Shiloh, Hannah excused herself after their meal and went to the temple of the Lord, where Eli, the priest sat next to its doorpost (see 1 Samuel 1:9). Hannah was heartbroken over her agony, and in tears she made a vow to the Lord: "O LORD of hosts, if you will indeed look on the affliction of your maidservant, and remember me, and not forget your maidservant, but will give to your maidservant a son, then I will give him to the LORD all the days of his life" (1 Samuel 1:11). How could Hannah do this, offer back to God a son for whom she had cried and prayed for years? Infertile women or mothers whose children die too soon often learn through their suffering a great truth that all parents must eventually understand. Children really do belong to God, not to us. When they come to us, we receive them as his gifts. We recall what happened to Sarah, another barren wife, when her focus was entirely on getting a child rather than waiting on God to keep his promise. She created great distress in her family. Hannah, through all her years of longing and praying for a child, learned that if she had a son, he would certainly be God's gift to her. There could be no other explanation. She believed the proper response to receiving this gift would be willingness to return the gift to him, with thanksgiving. This exchange of gifts lies at the heart of all liturgical sacrifices, right up to the Mass we celebrate today. God has given us the greatest of gifts—his very own Son for our salvation—and we return this gift by giving him ourselves, with thanksgiving.

Hannah prayed silently, from the heart, moving her lips soundlessly. As Fr. Damasus Winzen writes in *Pathways in Scripture*:

> Her prayer is the word of her heart (1:13). It is poured forth
> from the innermost center of her personality, which has been

torn open by her bitterness of soul (1:10). Nevertheless, her
prayer is not a mere drifting of the heart on the waves of
emotion. Her lips move (1:13), which means that her prayer
consists of definite, formulated thoughts.[29]

This prayer is a window into Hannah's soul. She referred to
herself three times as the Lord's *"maidservant."* Hers was a posture
of humility before him. She made no mention of how long she
had waited and prayed for a child, nor did she blame Peninnah
for her insults or Elkanah for his lack of understanding. There
was no whining in her request, no demand made of the Lord
because of her piety. She was willing to receive from him, not
grasp. In every way this prayer has the fragrance of a woman
who loved God from the heart and trusted him to be the only one
to whom her agony should be revealed.

Eli, the priest, watched Hannah's lips moving without any
sound. Thinking her to be drunk, he harshly rebuked her: *"How
long will you be drunken? Put away your wine from you"* (1 Samuel
1:14). Hannah had fled Peninnah's torment to seek solace in prayer
at the Temple, only to be met by insult and misunderstanding
from the priest there. Pain upon pain, how did she respond to
this? How would we respond? *"But Hannah answered, 'No, my
lord, I am a woman sorely troubled; I have drunk neither wine nor
strong drink, but I have been pouring out my soul before the LORD.
Do not regard your maidservant as a base woman, for all along I
have been speaking out of my great anxiety and vexation'"* (1 Samuel
1:15–16). Her response gives us another window into her soul.
In answer to the sting of Eli's judgment, Hannah was humble,
not defensive. She simply explained what she was doing without
any tone of rebuke or retaliation for his behavior. In fact, just as
she referred to herself in her prayer as the Lord's *"maidservant,"*

she called herself *"your maidservant"* to the rude priest. She gave the same respect to the Lord's priest as she gave to the Lord himself. Her meekness and honesty cut right through Eli's severe misjudgment of her: *"Go in peace,"* he said, *"and the God of Israel grant your petition which you have made to him"* (1 Samuel 1:17). He recognized her godly character instantly. Hannah received Eli's blessing as a word from the Lord to her, saying, *"'Let your maidservant find favor in your eyes.' Then the woman went her way and ate, and her countenance was no longer sad"* (1 Samuel 1:18).

What a remarkable visit to the temple this turned out to be for Hannah. She arrived in great pain, and she left in great peace. It is remarkable for another reason, as well. As Sarah Christmyer writes in *Becoming Women of the Word*:

> Hannah is the first person in the Old Testament who shows us we can throw ourselves on God, pour out our distress, and find comfort and help. Later, David will do the same, and he will give us words in the Psalms so we'll know how to do it, too. But—maybe it's the feminine genius at work in her, the woman's need for relationship—Hannah is the first whose prayer we hear, not as a leader concerned for the flock but as an ordinary person like [us]. She shows us that faith involves a deeply personal connection with God.[30]

Early the next morning, Hannah and her family *"worshipped before the Lord"* (1 Samuel 1:19), then went back home. She and Elkanah came together in the conjugal embrace, and *"the Lord remembered her, and in due time Hannah conceived and bore a son"* (1 Samuel 1:19–20). She called him Samuel, whose name meant, *"I have asked him of the Lord"* (1 Samuel 1:20). She nursed him, probably for three years, and when he was weaned, she and her family went back to the temple in Shiloh. There they offered the prescribed sacrifices (see 1 Samuel 1:24), and then they *"brought the child to Eli"* (1 Samuel 1:25). Hannah wanted to keep her vow: *"Oh, my lord ... I am the woman who was standing here in your presence, praying to the* LORD. *For this child I prayed; and the* LORD *has granted me my petition ... Therefore, I have lent him to the* LORD; *as long as he lives, he is lent to the* LORD*"* (1 Samuel 1:26–28). Although this could have been a scene of painful sorrow over their separation from their beloved son, Elkanah and Hannah then *"worshipped the* LORD*"* (1 Samuel 1:28).

There is great maternal poignancy in Hannah's words: *"As long as he lives, he is lent to the* LORD*"* She knew Samuel would never live with her again; he would grow up to do priestly and prophetic work for the Lord. She also knew in her heart that for *"as long as he lives"* she would be his mother, and he would be her son. The physical bond of proximity between them would end, but nothing could sever the maternal bond of love for her boy, now to be shared forever with the Lord. This is the confidence that lives in the heart of every priest's mother.

After Elkanah and Hannah *"worshipped the* LORD*"* at the temple, *"Hannah also prayed"* a song of praise to the Lord (see 1 Samuel 2:1–10). Once again, her prayer expresses her heart's deepest emotions. This time, however, joy permeates her soul rather than sorrow: *"My heart exults in the* LORD; *my strength is exalted in the* LORD*"* (1 Samuel 2:1). Her song goes on to describe how God works through reversals, as he had done for her, making her barren womb fruitful. Over and over, she sings about the deception of appearances—the mighty look strong, but it is the feeble who *"gird on strength"* (1 Samuel 2:4). Those who were *"full"* wind up hungry, while *"the hungry have ceased to hunger"* (1

Samuel 2:5). The song is shot through with confidence in God's power and care for his people: *"For the pillars of the earth are the Lord's, and on them he has set the world"* (1 Samuel 2:8). At the song's end, Hannah prophetically sings of a time in Israel when there would be a king rather than judges to rule, an *"anointed"* one whose power God would *"exalt."* St. Augustine has commented on this aspect of Hannah's song:

> Do you say that these are the words of a single weak woman giving thanks for the birth of a son? Can the mind of men be so much averse to the light of truth as not perceive that the sayings this woman pours forth exceed her measure? ... Unless perchance anyone will say that this woman prophesied nothing, but only lauded God with exulting praise on account of the son whom she had obtained in answer to prayer. What then does she mean when she says, ' ... *[T]he barren hath born seven and she that hath many children is waxed feeble?'* Had she herself born seven, although she had been barren? She had only one when she said that; neither did she bear seven afterwards, nor six ... And then, when as yet no one was king over that people, whence, if she did not prophesy, did she say what she puts at the end, *'He giveth strength to our kings, and shall exalt the horn of His Christ.'*[31]

St. Augustine suggested that although Hannah's song found fulfillment in the birth of Samuel in a literal sense, in its spiritual sense it pointed toward fulfillment in the royal throne of David and the ultimate Anointed One among David's descendants, the Messiah, Jesus Christ.

In singing her song, Hannah joined the growing list of women who raised their feminine voices in praise and thanksgiving for

God's goodness—his trustworthiness—in caring for his people. There is beautiful irony in this. In Eden, the Serpent won Eve over by casting doubt on God's character, suggesting he had lied to her about the fruit and convincing her he could not be trusted. It was a woman who was deceived by that lie, but that woman was followed by many women who sang the *truth* about God— his wisdom, love, power, and care of those whom he created. Those feminine voices filled the void left by Eve's silence in the Garden. What a sweet and welcomed sound it is!

Hannah's boy, Samuel, ministered with Eli, the priest, in Shiloh. She yearly made him *"a little robe"* (1 Samuel 2:19) to wear in his service there. She and Elkanah took it up to him when they offered their yearly sacrifices. Eli would bless them and say, *"The Lord give you children by this woman ... for the loan which she lent to the Lord"* (1 Samuel 2:20). The Lord did exactly that. Hannah went on to give birth to three sons and two daughters while her boy Samuel *"grew in the presence of the Lord"* (1 Samuel 2:21). Her willing sacrifice of her firstborn son to the Lord's service proved exceedingly fruitful. The once-barren woman was never without children again.

Hannah and Mary

In the Mass for Friday of the third week of Advent, Year A, the Church gives us as the First Reading Hannah's gift of Samuel to the priest at the temple in Shiloh; her prayer song as the Responsorial Psalm; and Mary's *Magnificat* as the Gospel reading. Here the Church testifies to how Hannah is a type of Mary.

The similarities between the prayer songs of Hannah and Mary are remarkable. Hannah's prayer begins, *"My heart exults in the Lord; my strength is exalted in the Lord ... There is none holy like the* LORD, *there is none besides you; there is no rock like our God"* (1 Samuel 2:1–2). Right away, this sounds familiar. Mary's *Magnificat* takes up words and themes of Hannah's song: *"My soul magnifies the Lord, and my spirit rejoices in God my Savior"* (Luke 1:46–47). Both go on to extol the greatness, the holiness of God. Both express personal joy over the impossible made possible. Both sing praises of God's character, for the wonderful reversals he has worked in human history. Both prayers contrast human pride, arrogance, and accomplishment with God's humbling action in raising the lowly, the powerless, and the empty to victory.

However, as we think more deeply about Hannah's story, we see many more beautiful hints of the mother to come who would one day sing a sister-song to hers.

First, Hannah's name means "grace" in Hebrew; Mary was addressed by an angel as *"full of grace"* (Luke 1:26). Hannah's story revealed her to be a quiet, humble woman describing herself as the Lord's *"maidservant"* who had found favor with God (see 1 Samuel 1:18). Mary's life revealed her to be a quiet, humble woman who described herself as a *"handmaid of the* LORD*"* (Luke 1:38, 48); she had *"found favor"* with God (Luke 1:30). Hannah's heart was broken by the pain of her infertility, the taunts of Peninnah, and her husband's lack of understanding. Still, she poured out her agony only to the Lord; even before the priest her prayer was silent, from the heart, heard only by the Lord. When Mary was confronted either by something wonderful (the nativity visit of the shepherds) or something painful (finding Jesus in the Temple after three anxious days), she had a similar quiet response: *"But Mary kept all these things, pondering them in her heart"* (Luke 2:19). Like Hannah, Mary sought the Lord's help to understand the events in her life in the silence of her heart with him. Both Hannah and Mary recognized that their sons truly belonged to the Lord. Hannah took Samuel to the priest at Shiloh, the place of worship, to keep her vow to lend him back to God. Mary heard of the Lord's claim on her Son's life from Simeon at the Jerusalem Temple when she and Joseph presented him as the Law required, and she heard it from her Son's own lips when she found him in the Temple, astounding all who heard him. Both women showed great faith and courage in releasing their beloved sons into the loving hands of God forever. Samuel grew *"in stature and in favor with the LORD and with men"* (1 Samuel 2:26). After Jesus went home from the Temple with Mary and Joseph, he *"increased in wisdom and in stature and in favor with God and man"* (Luke 2:52). Both their sons grew up to be priests and prophets, with Jesus being the fulfillment of the "anointed" king whom Hannah foretold in her prayer song. Both women were blessed with other children. Hannah bore five children after Samuel left her; Mary became the mother of St. John at the foot of the Cross, as well as all the others who would follow Jesus when he left her. There was marvelous fruit from the sacrifices they had made.

Is it any wonder that Mary is sometimes spoken of as "the new Hannah," who, in her gracious, humble life, fulfilled the hints Hannah gave of what grace looks like in a godly woman?

— *Pondering Hannah* —

Recall what we have learned about Hannah from her story:

- her uncomplaining ability to hold her tongue when treated harshly (by Peninnah), not understood (by her husband), or insulted (by the priest)
- her resolve to save all the words she wanted to utter about her pain for God's ears only
- her smooth constancy of character between who she was in prayer and who she was when confronted immediately afterwards by a difficult person
- her choice to turn to God alone for the healing of all that troubled her and not to allow the long years of suffering to embitter her
- her profound generosity in giving the gift of her son back to the Lord for lifelong service
- her tender, maternal love for Samuel, who was away from her physically but never out of her mind and heart
- her feminine voice raised in song to praise God's kindness not only to her but to all who are lowly and bereft
- in her prayer song, her impulse to spend her words on extolling God's character and actions in the world rather than on her own sorrows

What questions can Hannah's example of a woman of grace help us ask ourselves?

- How important to me is my own quiet humility in my life with God and others?
- Am I willing to reserve my words during difficulties for God's ears only?
- Am I the same woman in my daily life, especially when people or situations are difficult, as I am when I am praying?
- In my prayers, do I balance my petitions with profession of my trust in God's character—his goodness, wisdom, power, and love?
- Can I hold my tongue when treated harshly or when misunderstood or insulted, answering only with respectful humility and simple honesty?
- If I have suffered long years with a seemingly unsolvable problem, has my suffering taught me the humility to turn to God alone with it, or has it embittered me so that I regularly express my pain, frustration, or anger to others?
- Hannah's song revealed God's constant attention to the lowly, needy, and weak of this world; are my eyes and heart open to them, as well?
- Do I believe that sacrifices made for the Lord can bear wonderful fruit?

Are there any lingering impressions from Hannah's life that you do not want to forget? Perhaps you can write them down below.

Chapter Seven

Bathsheba—In the Time of the Royal Kingdom

"And the king rose to meet her and bowed down to her;
then he sat on his throne, and had a seat brought for
the king's mother; and she sat on his right."

—I Kings 2:19

Historical Context: Royal Kingdom (1050–930 BC)

In about 1050 BC, Israel made the transition from its chaotic life under the direction of a series of judges into a kingdom united under royal rule until 930 BC. The first king in this Royal Kingdom time period, Saul, who was anointed by Samuel, Hannah's son, eventually became so disobedient that the Lord removed him from the throne. Then, by God's direction, Samuel anointed a young shepherd boy, David, to rule as king in his place. David and his son Solomon reigned over an Israelite nation that rose to great heights in power, prestige, and influence among the nations that surrounded it. Because David was a man after God's own heart, as God once described him, the Lord made a covenant with David to secure his throne forever. The rightful successor to the throne of Israel would always be one of David's descendants. Jesus was the final and eternal King to fulfill God's promise, a descendant of David and of David's wife, Bathsheba. It is to her story, the story of the mother of a line of kings, that we now turn.

The Woman, Bathsheba

Not long after David was anointed king of a united Israel and God made covenantal promises to him of a throne that would last forever (see 2 Samuel 7:1–29), he made an unexpected departure from his habit of obedience to God in a life marked by trust and humility. *"In the spring of the year, the time when kings go forth to battle,"* David sent his army into battle, *"but David remained in Jerusalem"* (2 Samuel 11:1). We might wonder what prompted this violation of his kingly vocation. Perhaps the remarkable promises God made to secure his throne forever fed presumption in his heart. Perhaps he mistakenly thought he could do no wrong.

"It happened late one afternoon, when David arose from his couch and was walking upon the roof of the king's house, that he saw ... a woman bathing, and the woman was very beautiful" (2 Samuel 11:2). That woman was Bathsheba, the Hebrew wife of Uriah, the Hittite. He was a Gentile God-fearer who embraced his wife's religion and people. He also gave excellent military service in King David's special group of warriors, the *"mighty men"* (see 2 Samuel 23:39; 1 Chronicles 11:26, 41). When David *"arose from his couch"* to walk on his roof, it was a rising from a couch of luxury and power; it led to a great falling. David's leisure while the army was out fighting for him opened an occasion for lust, and his lust overtook him. *"So David sent messengers, and took her; she came to him, and he lay with her"* (2 Samuel 11:4).

Bathsheba had been bathing in her home, possibly in an

enclosed courtyard, on a hot day. She was not necessarily completely undressed. There is nothing in the Scriptural account to suggest that she was doing anything other than what it tells us: *"Now she was purifying herself from her uncleanness"* (2 Samuel 11:4). She was simply observing the Jewish ritual of cleansing herself after her monthly menstrual period. Generally, this occurred before ovulation, a fertile time in a woman's cycle. Physical contact with any blood made Jews ritually "unclean" since blood represented death, a contradiction of ritual cleanness or the life of holiness before God. We do not see any seductive culpability in Bathsheba. In her faithful obedience to Jewish law, she became a victim of David's unfaithful disobedience to it. That was only the beginning.

The words describing this episode are spare—David saw her, he sent for her, he took her, he lay with her. We must wonder what reaction Bathsheba had to all of this. No word of hers is recorded for us. Did she want to resist David's advances? If so, what opportunity would she have for that? He was the powerful king whom her husband served. Perhaps that left her feeling she had no choice but to obey. Others in Scripture had resisted sexual assault. Joseph, the son of Jacob who rose to prominence in Egypt, fled from the clutches of Potiphar's wife (see Genesis 39) and wound up in prison. Susanna, a noble Jewish wife who lived in the time of the Exile, was spied on by two lascivious elders of the community while she was bathing in her own private garden. They assaulted her, and she cried out for help. To shield themselves, they falsely accused her of adultery. It was only by a last-minute intervention in her trial by the prophet Daniel that she was spared a death sentence (see Daniel 13). What kept Bathsheba silent? A respected, beloved king, as David was in Israel, was certainly different from a lustful wife or corrupt elders. Although there is no suggestion of violence in this episode, it seems David used his position of power to get what he wanted from Bathsheba. When he was done with her, *"she returned to her house"* (2 Samuel 11:4).

In time, the consequences of David's sin began to ripen. First, he received word from Bathsheba: *"I am with child"* (2 Samuel 11:5). This left her in the terrible predicament of bearing a child that could not possibly be her husband's, since Uriah was out fighting in the king's army. She would be subject to the punishment of adultery—death. She let David know the problem he had created for them both.

David sprang into action when he got the news. He did not want the finger of accusation to point to him, the great new king of Israel. He plotted to make it seem that Uriah had fathered the child. He brought him in from fighting and told him to take his rest in his own home. Then, in an ironic twist, Uriah slept at the king's door instead of in his own bed with Bathsheba. When David asked him, the next day, why he had not gone home, Uriah said: *"The ark and Israel and Judah dwell in booths; and my lord [commander] Joab and the servants of my lord are camping in the open field; shall I then go to my house, to eat and to drink, and to lie with my wife?"* (2 Samuel 11:11). Uriah's devout obedience to his vocation for the honor of the God of Israel and his people, stood in sharp contrast to David's neglect of his own for the sake of his lust. Even when David insisted Uriah spend another day in Jerusalem so that he could get him drunk and perhaps lower his resistance to going home, the drunken Uriah stood firm. David's plan failed. Rather than recognizing his failure, David got desperate. He arranged for Uriah to return to the fighting and to be put in the front line, where the battle was fiercest. The soldiers around him would then pull back, leaving Uriah vulnerable to the enemy's wrath. That worked; Uriah died in the battle.

Meanwhile, Bathsheba had to stand by once again and let the powerful king make decisions that would deeply affect her life. When she learned of her husband's death, *"she made lamentation for her husband"* and mourned him (2 Samuel 11:26). When her mourning time was over, David sent for her, brought her to his house, and *"she became his wife, and bore him a son."* David thought he had finally solved the problem he created. *"But the thing that David had done displeased the Lord"* (2 Samuel 11:27).

We see from this last verse that in the Lord's eyes David was responsible for this mess. Not only had he used Bathsheba to satisfy his appetite, but he also deceived himself into believing that arranging the death of his own soldier was the answer to his troubles. Although he made Bathsheba his wife, was it love or lust that led him to it? Did he care more about his own reputation as a great and noble king than he did about his cruel abuse of two innocent people? Bathsheba knew the answers. She and Uriah had been faithful to the laws of Israel; they appear to have been a devout couple who loved each other. Bathsheba wept— lamented—over Uriah's death. What good could she possibly expect from a marriage conceived in such evil?

God sent the prophet Nathan to warn David of the consequences of his actions. He used a parable to pinpoint the exact nature of David's sin, in which a rich and powerful man took the beloved ewe lamb of a poor man, a lamb who *"was like a daughter to him"* (2 Samuel 12:3). David immediately recognized the wrong done by the rich man who, he said, deserved to die for what he had done and ought to make a *"fourfold"* restoration for his great sin (see 2 Samuel 12:5–6). Nathan then told him, *"You are the man!"* (2 Samuel 12:7).

We learn several things from David's encounter with Nathan. First, we see that the rich man in the parable used his power to get what he wanted. If we have wondered about Bathsheba's role in all of this, now we know. She was as innocent as the ewe lamb who had been loved and treasured by the poor man. Then, we hear David recognize that the sin of the rich man in the parable deserved punishment. When we read the rest of David's story in Scripture, we see in his own household the same sins he committed—lust, rape, deception, and murder—a "fourfold" punishment for his great sin.

David, upon hearing Nathan's parable and the scorching reproach God spoke to him (see 2 Samuel 12:7–14), fell into profound repentance. It is thought that during this time he wrote Psalm 51 (*"Have mercy on me, O God ... Wash me thoroughly from my iniquity, and cleanse me from my sin"*), the most famous of the penitential psalms in Scripture. To Nathan, he said, *"I have sinned against the LORD"* (2 Samuel 12:13). When confronted with his sin, he did not try to justify it or blame it on Bathsheba. Here, at last, we see the David we recognize from everything we know about him both before and after this episode.

Bathsheba, although clearly a victim in David's sin, may have had little joy in being David's wife, but we can well imagine what the birth of this little boy meant to her. There is no record of children born to her and Uriah; this boy was her firstborn. She knew he was completely innocent in the king's sin. We can also imagine the shock and grief she must have felt to learn that God would take him.

The child got sick. David gave himself completely to interceding for his life. He fasted; he lay prostrate before the Lord, begging for mercy on his son. His court officials tried to convince him to get up and eat, but David would have none of it. On the seventh day of his fasting, the child died. When he realized the Lord had not spared the boy, he got up, washed, and changed his clothes. Then, before eating, *"he went into the house of the LORD, and worshipped"* (2 Samuel 12:20). This is an important moment, a turning point in an otherwise dark, disappointing story. David, in his repentance over his sin, begged for the Lord's mercy. The child died. Bitterness and anger could have taken root in him, yet that is not what happened. David accepted God's just judgment. He was, again, a man after God's own heart (see 1 Samuel 13:14). After his great fall, his confession and repentance restored that divine light in his soul. He wanted to worship the God who had allowed his son to die. Only grace can explain such a thing in a man, and Bathsheba watched it all.

"Then David comforted his wife, Bathsheba" (2 Samuel 12:24). The man who walked into Bathsheba's room was a man entirely new to her. He *comforted* her. She was no longer a pawn in the nightmare he earlier created. Now, he loved her and cared about her in the grief that had overtaken her when their son died. She had witnessed the deep love he had for their son, how he recognized the great wrong he had done, how that drove him back to the God whom he had spurned by his sin. Perhaps this was the first real day of their lives as husband and wife, and it bore very good fruit.

Bathsheba gave birth to another son, Solomon, whose name in Hebrew means "peaceful." God promised to give *"peace and quiet to Israel in his days"* (1 Chronicles 22:9), a promise he kept.

Solomon's reign would be the golden age of Israel's history. At this time of the child's birth, God sent word to his parents that he loved the boy, so David *"called his name Jedidiah"* (see 2 Samuel 12:24–25), which means "beloved of the Lord." Think of what this word of the Lord's love for her son may have meant to Bathsheba. Perhaps it helped her understand how David could have gone straight to worship the Lord when he knew his first son had died. If David was able to trust God's love and wisdom again, this word of love from the Lord for her new son surely would have helped her to do that, too. She took it as a sign of her son's greatness before God. This woman could finally know true joy.

As the years went by, Nathan's prophecy over the house of David was fulfilled. David's kingship never fully recovered its former greatness, and there were great struggles and rivalries among his children as they grew into adulthood. When it came time for David to appoint a successor to his throne, Bathsheba approached him to remind him of a promise he made to make Solomon king after him: *"Bathsheba bowed and did obeisance to the king, and the king said, 'What do you desire?' She said to him, 'My lord, you swore to your maidservant by the* Lord *your God, saying, 'Solomon your son shall reign after me, and he shall sit upon my throne'"* (1 Kings 1:16–17). Nathan confirmed this, and David vowed to keep his promise. *"Then Bathsheba bowed with her face to the ground, and did obeisance to the king, and said, 'May my lord King David live forever!'"* (see 1 Kings 1:31).

When Solomon sat on the throne after David's death, he at first ruled as one "beloved of the Lord." He was known for building the magnificent Temple in Jerusalem, asking only for wisdom as God's gift, and expanding and strengthening Israel's position among the nations. Yet, there was still great unrest and rivalry in David's household. At one point, Solomon's treacherous half brother, Adonijah, approached Bathsheba with a request to advocate for him to the king so he could take a woman named Abishag as his wife. He was confident in her advocacy, because *"he will not refuse you"* (1 Kings 2:17). It is probable Bathsheba did not recognize the subtle treachery in this request. Abishag had been David's concubine. Marrying her was Adonijah's attempt to usurp royal prerogative.

Bathsheba went in to see Solomon: *"And the king rose to meet her, and bowed down to her; then he sat on his throne, and had a seat brought for the king's mother; and she sat on his right. Then she said, 'I have one small request to make of you; do not refuse me.' And the king said to her, 'Make your request, my mother; for I will not refuse you'"* (1 Kings 2:19–20). What a remarkable difference between her appearance before King Solomon, who was her son, and her appearance earlier before King David, who was her husband (see 1 Kings 1:16). Before David, Bathsheba had bowed; when she approached Solomon, he bowed to her. Here, the mother of the king was a queen, with royal power and her own seat at the king's right hand, always a symbol of royal authority. Solomon, in his wisdom, recognized the threat behind Adonijah's request and had to deny it, for the sake of unity in the kingdom. But the important feature for us to see is that Bathsheba's throne set the pattern for queenship in Israel, noted throughout the Old Testament. It was not the king's wife who was the queen (the king often had many wives), but instead it was his mother. The queen mother (*gebirah* in Hebrew) provided the continuity of the Davidic line that God had promised to preserve and thus laid the foundation for the future of God's people.

Bathsheba's story began in her powerlessness in the hands of a powerful man—David. Her relationship with David made her an adulteress, a widow, and the mother of a dead firstborn son. She must have felt the darkness around her life was complete. We do not know if she cried out to God for help, but it is likely she did as a pious Jewish woman. Did she pray for David, whom she could see had fallen into great sin? Did God answer her prayers in David's profound repentance and conversion? Did she ask God to give her strength to live in a way that pleased him in this life she had not sought or wanted?

We do not know the answers to these questions, but we do know that God worked a miraculous reversal for her. The woman who experienced a dramatic disruption in her life by great evil became the queen mother of Israel, the first but not the last in Israel's history to sit at the king's right hand in royal authority as both advocate of his subjects and counselor to him (see Proverbs 31:1). David did the grasping in Bathsheba's story; she did the receiving, of both bad and good. She is remembered as one of the four women named in Jesus' genealogy in the New Testament, where she is called *"the wife of Uriah"* (Matthew 1:6), not by her name. We can see this as underscoring the magnitude of David's sin against her, as well as God's willingness and power to magnificently redeem her from it.

Bathsheba and Mary

If we did not know Bathsheba's story, we might be tempted to cringe at the suggestion that she is a type of Mary. It would be easy to question how a woman who rose to royal power from such sordid circumstances could ever put us in mind of Mary, the holy mother of Jesus. However, when thinking about the woman Bathsheba as we have done, we understand that it is not so much by personality or character but by the *role* God gave her in Solomon's kingdom that she foreshadows Mary. We know Bathsheba to be yet another Old Testament woman who received something wonderful from God without grasping.

We saw her as King David's wife, when she humbly appeared before him as the mother of Solomon, calling herself *"maidservant"* (or "handmaid") and working to protect Solomon's right to David's throne, hotly contested among his other sons. She remembered the Lord's message of love for him at his birth, that he was beloved of the Lord, and his promise to give peace to the kingdom in his time. She interpreted that as God's promise that he would be king; she lovingly protected Solomon's right to the throne, promised by David, in her appearance before him. This was her first act of advocacy in her position as the king's wife. Later, as the king's mother, she sat in the newly established royal chair, a position acknowledged by Solomon when he *"bowed down to her"* as she approached him. Her power with the king was acknowledged even by Solomon's enemy, who asked for her advocacy on his behalf, knowing the king would not refuse her.

We can see that Queen Bathsheba is a fit model of Mary, the one who would become queen on earth and in heaven by virtue of being the mother of Jesus, the Messianic King in David's line. Mary, like Bathsheba, was elevated to her royal position in a most unlikely way, risking the charge of adultery, with its death penalty, by carrying a child not fathered by her betrothed husband, Joseph. She lived a quiet, humble life, calling herself a *"handmaid of the Lord"* (Luke 1:38). She was willing to advocate to her son on behalf of the hosts of the wedding at Cana who had run out of wine. She was full of love for her son and had the perception and boldness to make public his God-given role as the Messiah by precipitating his first public miracle there. Bathsheba was a good wife, a good mother, a royal queen. She received another son, beloved of the Lord, to fill the void left by the death of her firstborn. Mary was a good wife, a good mother, a royal queen. She too received another son, St. John, at the foot of the Cross, as well as all the other disciples of Jesus, to fill the void left by the departure of her firstborn.

Interestingly, there is simple biblical testimony to Mary's role as queen of Israel at the time of the Visitation. Mary visited her cousin, Elizabeth, shortly after the Annunciation. Upon her arrival there, Elizabeth, filled with the Holy Spirit, asked in delight, *"And why is this granted me, that the mother of my Lord should come to me?"* (Luke 1:43). As Edward Sri notes in *Rethinking Mary in the New Testament*, "While 'Lord' was often used … as a title for God, it could also refer to the royal son of David (2 Sam 24:21; 1 Kgs 1:13-47) and the future anointed king (Ps 110:1)."[32] Elizabeth was humbled by Mary's visit, the older woman by the younger, because she prophetically recognized that the baby in Mary's womb—his first earthly throne—was the new king of Israel. She knew this phenomenon made Mary the Queen Mother, making her marvel over Mary's visit.

Much later, in St. John's vision of heaven in Revelation 12, Mary appears as the mother of Jesus with a crown on her head—the queen of heaven. From the time of the Visitation to eternity, Mary was and always will be her Son's queen mother. Bathsheba, in her life of lights and shadows, is the first woman in Scripture who teaches us that the *"woman"* God promised in Genesis 3 would not only be a mother-warrior, she would also be queen.

— Pondering Bathsheba —

In our day, David's lustful grasp of Bathsheba would be called rape. Fortunately, in our day women can and do speak out about sexual wrongs committed against them. We also have strong voices of advocacy for children who are similarly abused. We can be thankful that our day is very different from the time in which Bathsheba lived.

However, for all the progress we have made in exposing this kind of sexual misbehavior, we are not free from it. Ours could be described as an age of constant, pervasive sexual arousal. In that kind of culture, there are always victims, both vocal and silent. Assaults can sometimes be physical, even violent. They can sometimes come through quiet manipulation of emotions or circumstances. People who have some type of power over us can use that power against us to get what they want and keep us silent. Some of us may be just such victims, and sadly we know that sometimes both men and women can be perpetrators, too.

If we have any of this in our past, can we let Bathsheba's story shed some light on what must often feel like a shadow of darkness from which we are never really free?

- Have you been a victim of someone else's unwanted sexual advances? Are you ever plagued by guilt over what happened even though you were not guilty of anything? Can you work to see yourself as the "ewe lamb" in Nathan's story, innocent in God's eyes, when phantom guilt tries to float through you?

- Have you ever manipulated someone else sexually to get what you wanted from him or her? When David understood the depth of the wrong he had done both to Bathsheba and to God, he experienced profound repentance and confession; God forgave him and gave him a fresh start in his life of faith. The sacrament of Reconciliation is exactly the place for us to do that. Do you need its wonderful graces now?

Although Bathsheba had been a victim, by God's grace that did not define her life. She went from utter helplessness as the wife of a man she had not chosen as her husband to a position of royal authority and power as the queen mother of Israel. Her past did not define her future. She became an ancestor of Jesus, the Messiah.

- If there is something in your past that keeps you feeling like a victim, can you let God's goodness as he revealed it in Bathsheba's life wash it away?

Are there any lingering impressions from Bathsheba's life that you do not want to forget? Perhaps you can write them down here or in your own journal.

Chapter Eight

The Desperate Widow and the Prophet Elisha—In the Time of the Divided Kingdom

"Your maidservant has nothing in the house,
except a jar of oil."

—2 Kings 4:2

Historical Context: Divided Kingdom (930–722 BC)

The glory of Israel that characterized the reigns of David and Solomon did not last long; its dissolution covered the period from 930 BC to 722 BC, the time period of the Divided Kingdom. Just as David sinned and brought trouble to his household, Solomon sinned, even more grievously than his father had, with devastating consequences. He amassed great wealth, taxed the people heavily to support his vast army, and married hundreds of wives, many of whom were pagans. As if that were not enough, he built temples to his wives' pagan gods, allowing worship of them in Israel. Consequently, when Solomon died, the united kingdom was ripped apart. Because of the harsh taxation his son, Rehoboam, levied on the people, a breakaway rebellion developed led by a man named Jeroboam. They established themselves in the northern part of the country; the new "nation" consisted of ten of Israel's tribes. It became the Northern Kingdom of Israel with its own throne, temple, and capital in Samaria. The Davidic line of kings continued in the Southern Kingdom of Judah, with the tribes of Judah and Benjamin and the Levites.

As could be expected, the Northern Kingdom, Israel, was plagued by rampant covenant infidelity, including idolatry, disregard for the Law of Moses, and cruel, unjust treatment of the poor. God sent many prophets to Israel to warn the people about their disobedience and to call them back to faithfulness to God, who loved them. Two great prophets, Elijah and Elisha, did miraculous works to arouse Israel out of its deadly slumber and return the people to the Lord. But eventually, their hearts were so hardened, especially under the influence of a succession of evil kings, that God allowed one of the curses Moses pronounced on this kind of iniquity to fall upon them—exile (see Leviticus 26:14–33; Deuteronomy 28:15–68). In 722 BC, the Assyrians conquered Israel, taking many of its people into an exile from which they never returned. Additionally, the Assyrians settled pagan foreigners in their place in Samaria who intermarried with the Israelites left behind.

However, in this time, the darkest period of Israel's history thus far, we find a widow whose story of faithful obedience shines brightly with prophetic light.

The Desperate Widow

During the time of Elisha's ministry as a prophet in Israel, we meet a widow in desperate straits. Hers is such a small, brief, and seemingly insignificant story that she is never named. Her husband, a devout man who had been one of the *"sons of the prophets*" (2 Kings 4:1) died suddenly, leaving her and her two sons in great debt. The "sons of the prophets" were schools of men being trained by a head prophet, called "father," to do prophetic work. Both Elijah and Elisha had such "sons." Elisha had been the "father" to this widow's husband. Now the widow sought Elisha's help: "*You know that your servant* [her husband] *feared the* LORD, *but the creditor has come to take my two children to be his slaves*" (2 Kings 4:1). The widow knew Elisha to be a holy man and a miracle worker who had received a "*double portion*" of the spirit of Elijah (see 2 Kings 2:9, 15). Since the widow had no money to pay her debt, the creditor demanded she give him her sons as slaves to clear it. She needed cash quickly, and plenty of it. Does it surprise us that she expected Elisha to help her? He had done many miracles in Israel—raised the dead, healed the sick, fed the hungry, made an infertile womb fruitful—but he hadn't produced volumes of money, which is what she needed. There is an element of our own surprise in his first response to her: "*What shall I do for you?*" (2 Kings 4:2). Then, he asked her what she had in her house. Maybe he planned to suggest she sell something to get the quick cash for her creditor. "*Your maidservant has nothing in the house, except a jar of oil*" (2 Kings 4:2). Now, we begin to understand just how desperate this widow was—she had already sold *all* her possessions. Her house was empty, nothing in it, except one jar of oil.

Elisha realized he had little with which to work. He told her, "*Go outside, borrow vessels of all your neighbors, empty vessels, and not too few. Then, go in, and shut the door upon yourself and your sons, and pour into all these vessels* [your oil], *and when one is full, set it aside*" (2 Kings 4:3–4). What do we think the widow would make of a plan that required her to gather as many empty vessels as she could from neighbors (and what would they think of such a strange request?) and fill them all with the oil she had in her single jar at home? Even if it sounded far-fetched to her, we know what she did. *"So, she went from him and shut the door upon herself and her sons; and as she poured, they brought vessels to her"* (2 Kings 4:5). In her obedience to Elisha's improbable plan, she discovered a miracle—that single jar of oil kept filling jar after jar without running dry. She and her sons presided over a remarkable multiplication of the valuable oil in their empty little house. Imagine their delight as it must have slowly dawned on them how this miraculous oil could save them from their poverty. When the widow requested the next vessel be brought to her for filling, the sons told her, *"There is not another"* (2 Kings 4:6). With that, *"the oil stopped flowing"* (2 Kings 4:6). She reported this news to Elisha, who told her, *"Go, sell the oil and pay your debts, and you and your sons can live on the rest"* (2 Kings 4:7). Not only would the widow have enough money to pay off her creditor, saving her sons from slavery, there would be enough money left over for them to live comfortably, without fear of poverty again. Elisha's miracle had worked a *superabundance* of riches for this widow, more than what she requested or needed. It was a stunning reversal for a woman whose name we never know, who is never mentioned again in Scripture. Nevertheless, we find her story still speaks to us.

The Widow and Mary

How can such an anonymous, obscure woman, living in a very troubled time in Israel's history, be a type of Mary? As small as her story is, perhaps we could see a suggestion of the answer to that question right away in the story's brief details.

The widow asked the holy man, Elisha, for help. His answer for the help she needed may have surprised her. It would require her to fill many borrowed vessels with what would become miraculous oil. The bounty of that oil not only paid off the widow's debt, but it also provided her and her sons with freedom from future debt. The solution to the widow's problem went beyond merely "good"; it was "the best."

Now, we should be able to see how a desperate widow who lived so many centuries earlier can speak to us of another mother (probably a widow, too), Mary, who approached another holy man, Jesus, for help in a desperate situation.

The scene is the wedding at Cana (see John 2:1–11). Mary noticed that the wedding hosts had run out of wine. In our day, this would not seem like a desperate situation. In that time and culture, however, a failure in this significant social event, evident to the whole community, would have brought shame and social stigma upon them for a long time to come. Mary saw that they needed plenty of wine, very quickly, to avoid that kind of suffering. She took the problem to Jesus.

What did she expect him to do? As soon as we recognize the strangeness of her expectation that Jesus would solve the wine shortage, we should begin to wonder if there is more to this episode than first meets the eye. What was it about Jesus and his disciples being present at this wedding feast that stirred Mary into action? The answer begins simply: she was his mother; she knew exactly who he was, Israel's long-awaited Messiah. She knew God was his Father; he was divine. She would have known from her long familiarity with Scripture that in the Old Covenant, God described himself as "husband" to Israel, his "bride" (see Isaiah 54:5; Jeremiah 3:20; Hosea 2:16, 19–20). Later, in his public ministry, Jesus described himself as the Bridegroom of the New Covenant people (see Matthew 9:15). Was Mary thinking about this Old Testament history as she watched her son and his friends enjoying themselves at a wedding feast? The Jews in that day expected that when the Messiah appeared, wine and the joy it can produce would flow freely (see Joel 2:19; Isaiah 25:6; 55:1). Did she think that her son was truly the Bridegroom there, the one responsible for providing the wine? Is that why she referred the problem to him? Jesus had come from God to us because all creation lacked the wine of freedom, the joy that was lost at the Fall. We were all in a desperate situation, in great poverty—not of money or wine but of life itself.

When Mary took the problem to Jesus, we can suspect she understood this moment in its greater significance. We see her step into her heroic moment, as Jesus' helper in the great redemptive work she shared with him. She asked Jesus for a miracle, without saying anything more than *"they have no wine"* (John 2:3). Only a miracle could solve this wine problem; only the true Bridegroom of Israel could perform it. We can see that Jesus at first registered some surprise when Mary approached him with the problem: *"O woman, what have you to do with me?"* (John 2:4). This was not a rejection of her concern, which would have been a violation of the commandment to honor parents. This was an idiomatic Hebrew way of inquiring what was being asked of him. It is like Elisha's first response to the widow: *"What shall I do for you?"* (2 Kings 4:2). Jesus called his mother *"woman."* This could suggest that in that moment, he saw her not simply as mother but as the *"woman"* of Genesis 3:15 who would help him in their definitive battle against God's enemy, the Devil. Because up to this point in his life, Jesus had not performed any public miracles, the battle was in its early stage. All that was about to change.

Jesus understood what Mary was suggesting when she simply said to him, *"They have no wine."* She expected him to work a miracle to provide it. A miracle worked in public, seen by both his disciples and all the servants through whose hands it would be worked, would be the first foray into a battle that would lead directly to his death. That is why he spoke the words that can appear unrelated to the issue at hand: *"My hour has not yet come"* (John 2:4). His *"hour"* is described in *The Ignatius Catholic Study Bible* this way:

> "At the historical level ... the 'hour' is the time when Christ passes through the agonies of betrayal and bodily torment, finally mounting the Cross out of love for the Father and as a sacrifice for our salvation. This 'hour' of Christ's humiliation and death is in John's Gospel the 'hour' of his exaltation that becomes the source of everlasting life for the world."[33]

Jesus' response to Mary provokes a question: Would he have spoken this way to her if she had no idea what his *"hour"* meant? Later in his ministry, Jesus often told his disciples about his *"hour,"* describing it in detail (see Matthew 16:21–22), but it was completely lost on them. They did not understand what he meant. Mary, however, was told by Simeon as he held the infant Jesus in his arms in the Temple that her Son would be a *"sign that is spoken against"* (Luke 2:34) in Israel and a *"light ... to the Gentiles"* (Luke 2:32) outside of it. Both he and she would know the piercing wound of a sword through their souls (see Luke 2:35). All of that would serve the purpose for which Jesus was born, as Simeon exclaimed to God: *"My eyes have seen your salvation which you have prepared in the presence of all peoples, a light for revelation to the Gentiles and for glory to your people Israel"* (Luke 2:30–32). Jesus' *"hour"* would be the source of salvation for God's "two sons," the Jews and the Gentiles (all non-Jews). Mary, like the desperate widow centuries before her, was able to ask for the miracle that would lead to freedom from the slavery of sin and death for his "two sons." She expected him to do it, as she turned to the servants and said, *"Do whatever he tells you"* (John 2:5).

When Mary heard Jesus speak his instructions to the servants—*"Fill the jars with water"* (John 2:7)—did her mind flash back to the unnamed widow in our story who had to fill many vessels with oil to save her two sons? The widow's obedience to the strange instructions from the holy man, Elisha, saved her sons from slavery. Mary encouraged the servants to obey *"whatever"* Jesus would tell them to do. Perhaps she expected it would seem strange to them, too. After the water had turned to wine, enough to provide drink to all the wedding guests, Mary would have heard the wine steward congratulate the bridegroom on its exceeding quality: *"You have kept the good wine until now"* (John 2:10). The wine was not just good, it was the best. Of course, the bridegroom had not done anything, but he benefited greatly from what Jesus had done for him. That is the essence of grace— God does for us what we cannot do for ourselves. It was Jesus, the Bridegroom of God's people, who had enriched the wine into a *superabundance* of quality and delight. Did this knowledge move Mary to remember the miraculous multiplication of oil in the desperate widow's story that meant a superabundance of riches for her family?

The story of the unnamed widow and the holy man Elisha is so fleeting it could easily slip away into obscurity within the much larger history of Israel. However, there is good reason to believe that for Mary it was, instead, a treasured story of how a desperate situation can turn into a source of unexpected blessing through one woman's request of a holy man whose intervention changed everything. Mary spoke to Jesus about a need much greater than wine for a wedding. She spoke to him on behalf of all of us in great poverty who need the riches only God can give, the blessing of salvation. It was time for them to begin their battle to gain it, even though it meant great suffering for them both. Out of compassion for God's people, her mother's heart spoke out on our behalf. She is still doing that for us.

— Pondering the Widow —

Our only contact with the widow in our story came in the midst of her crisis. We know nothing of her life before or after this episode. Is our exposure to her too limited to hear her speak to us? If our lives have never been touched by a crisis, a desperate situation from which we see no way out—or if we expect they never will—then we can let the widow's small story remain small. However, we are probably wiser than that. As Scripture tells us, "*man is born to trouble as the sparks fly upward*" (Job 5:7). It is inevitable that in this life troubles will come to us, both large and small. It would be good for us to pay attention to whatever this anonymous woman, a type of Mary, can teach us.

When the widow realized that her husband's sudden death plunged her into extreme poverty, she first did what she could to solve her problem. Before she went to Elisha, she sold everything in her house with the hope of getting enough money to pay her debts. Perhaps she was able to pay off some of them, but when the money was gone, one creditor remained. He demanded payment in flesh and blood—her two sons would become his slaves. That alone would clear the debt. So, it was the threat to her sons that turned her predicament into a crisis. When she realized what was at stake, she knew she needed help. She took the problem to the holy man, Elisha, whom she knew could work miracles. No more trying to figure out the solution to her problem for herself.

- Is there a lesson here for us in our desperate situations, when we have done all we can to solve a problem that will not go away? Do we have eyes to see what is at stake in the troubles that come our way? When we understand our great need and our poverty, do we take it to Jesus with confidence he can help us, as Mary did at Cana?

When the widow told Elisha about her great debt and the peril her sons faced, she did not heap blame on her dead husband for his financial management of their household. How did they get into such enormous debt? We do not know. Her husband had been a devout man, a disciple in Elisha's "*sons the prophets*." Had his pious involvement with Elisha distracted him from taking better care of his money? We cannot know this, but we can know that the widow did not blame anyone in angry words for her problem (not even the creditor!). All that mattered to her when she went to see Elisha was that she needed his help.

- Is there a lesson here for us if we suffer consequences of the bad choices or behavior of others? Can we let go of recrimination and stay focused on all that matters—we need God's help?

Although the widow had only one jar of oil left in her house, it was enough for God to deliver her and her sons from disaster.

- Is there a lesson here for us about how God can use something small in our poverty to deliver us and those we love from disaster when we go to him with our need?

The widow was delivered from her problem superabundantly. She went to Elisha impoverished; when she left him after the miracle, she went away rich.

- Is there a lesson here for us to help us believe that God can make even our suffering and our emptiness fruitful when we trust him with our crisis?

Are there any lingering impressions from the widow's life that you do not want to forget? Perhaps you can write them down here or in your own journal.

....

....

....

....

....

....

....

....

....

Chapter Nine

Esther—In the Land
of the Exile

"I have heard from the books of my ancestors that you
liberate all those who are pleasing to you, O LORD ... assist
me, who am all alone and have no one but you."

—Esther 14:11

Historical Context: Exile (722–538 BC)
*See the historical note at the end of the chapter.

After the fall of the Northern Kingdom of Israel in 722 BC, the
Southern Kingdom of Judah gradually succumbed to the same
covenant infidelity that led to Israel's destruction. Although
there were occasional good kings (namely, Hezekiah and Josiah)
who tried to heed the warnings of the prophets God sent to
them and reform the people, their efforts were not enough to
overcome the extreme wickedness of bad kings who sat on
David's throne. Manasseh, for example, was guilty of idolatry
and even child sacrifice. When the people thoroughly hardened
their hearts against the voice of the Lord, they were given the
severe punishment of exile for the sake of their rehabilitation.
In 586 BC, the Babylonians destroyed the city of Jerusalem,
including Solomon's magnificent Temple, and carted off most of
the inhabitants into exile in Babylon.

The darkness over God's holy land lasted until 538 BC, when the Persian king (the Persians displaced the Babylonians as rulers of the empire), Cyrus, allowed the Jews to return to their homeland. A whole generation of Jews grew up far from the Holy Land; far from the liturgical worship their ancestors had known and lost; but not, providentially, far from God, who loved them still. Even after this dark period in the history of God's people officially came to an end and the Jews began to return to the Holy Land, some remained in Persia. Here we meet two Jews living in exile whose story is full of twists and turns; it is threaded with delightful irony and grand reversals. It helps us see, even *"in bitter slavery"* (Esther 14:8), all was not lost for God's people.

Note: Some portions of the book of Esther originally existed only in Greek; the rest of the book was written in Hebrew. This can cause the reader some confusion, because many Catholic Bibles have an unusual numbering of the chapters. Ascension's *Great Adventure Catholic Bible* describes it this way in a note:

> The disarrangement of the chapter and verse order is due to the insertion of the deuterocanonical portions in their logical place in the story of Esther, as narrated in the Greek version from which they are taken ...
>
> In the old Vulgate [the Latin version of the Bible translated or adapted by St. Jerome from older Latin, Hebrew, or Aramaic versions] these portions were placed by Jerome immediately after the Hebrew text of Esther, regardless of their logical position ... Hence they came to be numbered 10:4–16:24.[34]

Some Catholic Bibles retain this chapter and verse numbering, even though the Greek portions are placed within the chronological flow of the story.

The Woman, Esther

In the book of the Old Testament named after her, we meet a beautiful young Jewish virgin, Esther, and her uncle and guardian, Mordecai. "[Mordecai] *had brought up Hadassah* [her Hebrew name], *that is Esther, the daughter of his uncle, for she had neither father nor mother; the maiden was beautiful and lovely, and when her father and her mother died, Mordecai adopted her as his own daughter*" (Esther 2:7). Mordecai was a royal official. One day, in the course of his duties as servant of the king, he overheard two palace eunuchs plotting to assassinate King Ahasuerus (sometimes called Artaxerxes in Greek). He told the king of the plot, thus saving his life. His loyal service was noted in the royal records, but he was never officially rewarded for what he had done.

One day the king decided to hold a lavish banquet for his high officials in the city of Susa, one of the capitals of the Persian Empire. He commanded his queen, Vashti, to enter the feast so he could show off her great beauty to his guests. This was against court etiquette, which kept the queen hidden away from public view. Vashti refused to appear, probably because of this custom, and because she didn't want to be paraded in front of a large group of leering men. Her refusal caused the king embarrassment and some confusion. He consulted with his advisors about what to do. They told him to depose Vashti, lest her example infect all the other women of the empire with similar insubordination. Not only did Vashti lose her crown, but a royal edict was sent out to all the people commanding that "*all women will give honor to their husbands, high and low*" (Esther 12:20).

Later, the king's advisors suggested he begin a search for a new queen. Accordingly, he called together all the most beautiful virgins throughout his realm, from whom he would choose the one who pleased him the most; she would wear the royal crown. Esther's remarkable beauty caught the attention of the officials sent out to search for the virgins: *"So when the king's order and his edict was proclaimed, and when many maidens were gathered in Susa, the capital ... Esther also was taken into the king's palace"* (Esther 2:8). This does not appear to have been a voluntary or sought-after participation in the king's beauty contest. Virgin women who were well-known for their beauty in their communities simply got rounded up and taken away.

The maidens were put in the charge of a court eunuch, Hegai, for their year-long preparation to appear before the king. The first hint that Esther's beauty was more than just her physical appearance comes from Hegai's reaction to her when they met: *"The maiden pleased him and won his favor; and he quickly provided her with her ointments and her portion of food ... and advanced her and her maids to the best place in the harem"* (Esther 2:9). Was it simply Esther's remarkable beauty that attracted Hegai's notice and won special treatment for her? Recall that Esther was described earlier as *"beautiful and lovely"* (Esther 2:7). This could seem to be a redundancy of meaning for the sake of emphasis, but it is not. These two words in Hebrew are different. As Sarah Christmyer notes, "The first descriptor in Hebrew proclaims her physical beauty. The second is the word used seven times in Genesis 1 when God calls his creation *'good.'* She was perfection itself; beautiful inside and out."[35] No wonder Hegai found Esther irresistible.

In all this time, on the counsel of Mordecai, Esther did not make known that she was a Jew (see Esther 2:10). This was probably because Mordecai sensed the tenuous position of the Jews, foreigners in exile, within the Persian Empire. He thought it best for them to keep a low profile about their background. That worked, but only for a time.

All the maidens, after their prolonged cosmetic preparation, had to appear individually before the king so he could make his choice. When it was Esther's turn, *"the king loved Esther more than all the women, and she found grace and favor in his sight more than all the virgins, so that he set the royal crown on her head and made her queen instead of Vashti"* (Esther 2:17). The king had only to look at Esther to be completely overcome by her remarkable appearance. No matter how gorgeous the other maidens were who appeared before him, no one could match the luminous vision of this simple Jewish virgin. The king was so delighted in his new queen that he held a feast in her honor and *"granted a remission of taxes to the provinces and gave gifts with royal liberality"* (Esther 2:18). So, without any effort or grasping on her part, Esther was elevated out of her small, humble life to be queen of an empire, an elevation that spilled over into superabundance of goodness to others throughout the realm.

What might Esther and Mordecai have thought of this sudden and unexpected change in their lives? During her year-long cosmetic confinement, waiting to appear before the king, did Esther think of herself as a prisoner of unwanted circumstances? She had been made part of the king's harem; if he had not chosen her as his queen, she would have been returned to the harem, never able to leave. Surely this was not how the young virgin dreamed of her future. If she resented this strange turn of events in her life, however, she did not show it. Her appearance was not tainted by inner unhappiness. On the contrary, her beauty, both inside and out, won over Hegai and the king. Although we do not know much about this

young woman at this point in her story, we already find much
to admire in her.

Mordecai, her uncle who loved her as his own daughter,
must likewise have been surprised by her elevation to her royal
position. We know he worried about her welfare when she was
taken from him: *"Every day Mordecai walked in front of the court of
the harem, to learn how Esther was and how she fared"* (Esther 2:11).
Did he do this because he was hopeful she would be chosen by the
king to be queen, or was he worried about how a young Jewish
girl would manage in an environment so full of temptation or,
perhaps, danger?

If he worried about her, he had good cause. There was a man
in the king's court named Haman; he served in the position of
the king's second-in-command. His position of authority was so
high that the king required all the court officials who entered
the palace gate to bow down to him (see Esther 3:2). Mordecai
refused to do this, although he was continually pressed to
obey. As a Jew, he would not "bow down" to another human
being; he would only give this kind of reverence to the Lord
(see Esther 13:13–14). Mordecai knew, too, that Haman was
a descendant of the ancient Amalekites, a tribe of people who
were relentless enemies of Israel throughout their history. When
Mordecai could no longer hide the reason for his resistance to
the king's command, he finally explained that as a Jew, he could
not do obeisance to the descendant of his enemies. His public
acknowledgement of being a Jew ignited a raging conflagration
of Haman's anger, a fire that knew no bounds.

Haman, in his fury, urged the king to put to death not only
Mordecai but *all* the Jews living in the empire as well. He used
suspicion of their disloyalty to the king, a threat to the unity

and stability of the empire, to justify this genocide. Upon their destruction, Haman would put *"ten thousand talents of silver"* (Esther 3:9) into the king's coffers. The king, trusting his second-in-command's advice and impressed by his bribe, issued the order. Thus both Mordecai and Esther, along with all their people, faced a royal death sentence.

When Mordecai learned of the king's decree, he went into public mourning. He was not alone in this: *"In every province, wherever the king's command ... came, there was great mourning among the Jews, with fasting and weeping and lamenting, and most of them lay in sackcloth and ashes"* (Esther 4:3). Mordecai sent word to Esther, urging her *"to go to the king, to make supplication to him and entreat him for her people"* (Esther 4:8). He reminded her of her *"days of ... lowliness,"* (Esther 4:8) when he was the only one to care for her. She needed him then; he and all her people needed her now: *"Beseech the Lord and speak to the king concerning us and deliver us from death"* (Esther 4:8).

Esther quickly answered her uncle's message with her own bad news. No one, not even the queen, could enter the king's presence to talk to him except by invitation, upon pain of death. She knew from what happened to Vashti how the king treated insubordination. Only those to whom the king extended his golden scepter would be allowed to live. Mordecai sent word right back to Esther, with a sober warning: *"Think not that in the king's palace you will escape any more than all the other Jews"* (Esther 4:13). He wanted her to realize the urgency of the trouble that threatened them. Then, he wisely guided her to reflect on all that had happened in her life: *"And who knows whether you have not come to the kingdom for such a time as this"* (Esther 4:14). His wise words shot a shaft of light on Esther; they gave her much-needed clarity, enabling her to see exactly what she must do. She sent word back to Mordecai: *"Go, gather all the Jews to be found in Susa, and hold a fast on my behalf, and neither eat nor drink for three days, night or day. I and my maids will also fast as you do. Then I will go to the king, though it is against the law, and if I perish, I perish"* (Esther 4:16).

We are now finally hearing Esther speak in her own words. Here, in this time of crisis, we see who she really was—a devout Jewish woman who felt deep solidarity with her people. She knew that before she undertook the dangerous work she had to do to save them she needed their fasting and prayers. When she and her people had done all the preparation required, she would go to the king on their behalf, even if it meant her death. A brave, pious heart beat in the breast of Queen Esther.

As promised, Esther threw herself into fasting and prayer, a prayer that gives us a window into this courageous woman's soul. There, we get an answer to a question we pondered earlier: What did Esther make of her elevation from *"lowliness"* to royal grandeur? In her ardent prayer, she told God exactly how she felt about it: *"You know of my necessity—that I abhor the sign of my proud position, which is upon my head on the days when I appear in public. I abhor it like a menstruous rag, and I do not wear it on the days when I am at leisure"* (Esther 14:16). She hated being the queen of a pagan empire. Then, she went on: *"Your servant has had no joy since the day I was brought here until now, except in you, O Lord God of Abraham"* (Esther 14:18). Queen Esther, always a vision of loveliness—goodness—to those who saw her was animated by joy in God alone. Neither her circumstances nor her feelings about them could rob her of this serenity. *"O God, whose might is over all, hear the voice of the despairing, and save us from the hands of evil doers. And save me from my fear!"* (Esther 14:19). Esther knew that God is *"over all,"* that he would hear and respond to the cry of despair from his people. She also knew she could be completely honest with him—she was absolutely terrified by what lay ahead. Her trust and confidence in God, the only source of joy she had in her royal life, did not remove the dread of what he now required of her. She suffered real agony as she faced the threat of death. Nevertheless, she was able to say, *"If I perish, I perish."*

After her three days of fasting, Esther *"clothed herself in splendid attire"* (Esther 15:1) for her visit to the king. *"She was radiant with perfect beauty, and she looked happy, as if beloved, but her heart was frozen with fear"* (Esther 15:5). Now, of course, we know from Esther's prayer that it was solely her trust in God that graced her with *"perfect beauty."* She knew that she was, indeed, *"beloved"* by him with a love that infused her countenance with happiness. Her human heart, however, still felt the chill of terror.

When she and her maids first entered the king's presence, he was angry. The look he gave her caused her to faint, an indication of how thoroughly afraid she was. *"Then God changed the spirit of the king to gentleness, and in alarm he sprang from his throne and took her in his arms until she came to herself"* (Esther 15:8). Thinking she feared only for her own life, he assured her that her royal position spared her (see Esther 15:8–9). He extended his golden scepter, asking what she wanted of him. Her answer might surprise us: *"If it please the king, let the king and Haman come this day to a dinner that I have prepared for the king"* (Esther 5:4).

What? We would expect Esther to ask the king to spare her people from death in answer to his question. Instead, she wanted the enemy to dine with the king at her table. Perhaps this looks like a loss of nerve. Yet as this story unfolds, the dinner—calm, amicable—sets the stage for a series of remarkable reversals that result in a resolution for Esther, Mordecai, and all their people that far exceeds expectation or even imagination.

As the three of them drank wine that night at dinner, the king asked Esther again what she wanted him to do for her. She asked only that both men return the following night to dine with her once more. Esther did not rush her serious request. Did she want to catch Haman off guard with the hospitality she offered? Did she hope Haman would observe firsthand the deep affection the king had for her, a Jew? Did she simply sense the time was not quite right for her to reveal what she truly needed from the king? Whatever the cause, her caution in using her position in the royal court suggests Esther was wise and sensitive to her situation. Carefully observing the men at her table—reading the signs of their demeanor, listening to the words they spoke, understanding the atmosphere their conversation created—she timed her action with precision. She needed one more night of togetherness for her next step.

Esther could not have known what would transpire in the twenty-four-hour delay. Haman left the dinner party *"joyful and glad of heart"* (Esther 15:9), probably the result of both its conviviality and its easy flow of wine. This happy state of mind was sharply interrupted when Haman spied Mordecai at the palace gate, who still refused to bow to him. Haman was furious, but he *"restrained himself"* (Esther 15:10), and he went home to vent his rage to his wife. He told her that although he held the second-highest position of honor in the king's court—and he used the intimate dinner he had enjoyed with the king and queen as evidence—he could never be happy if Mordecai sat at the king's gate, refusing to show him honor. His wife and friends suggested a solution: he should build a *"gallows fifty cubits high ... and in the morning tell the king to have Mordecai hanged upon it"* (Esther 15:14). Then, he could go his merry way to Esther's dinner party that night. Haman considered this to be excellent advice; he had the gallows built.

Also on that night, the king had some difficulty getting to sleep, so he called for the royal records to be brought in and read to him. In them was the account of how Mordecai once saved his life from an assassination plot, yet there was no record of his ever being rewarded for that important service. The king wanted to rectify this omission. As it happened, when the king inquired who was in the court to advise him about what to do, *"Haman had just entered the outer court of the king's palace to speak to the king about having Mordecai hanged on the gallows that he had prepared for him"* (Esther 6:4). The king called for him and asked, *"What shall be done to the man whom the king delights to honor?"* (Esther 6:6). Of course, Haman thought the king meant this honor for him, so he described a lavish outpouring of royal splendor on this man. He would wear the king's own robes and crown, ride the king's own horse, and be paraded through the city square with the highest accolades (see Esther 6:7–9). Imagine Haman's shock when he heard these words from the king: *"Make haste ... and do so to Mordecai the Jew who sits at the king's gate. Leave out nothing that you have mentioned"* (Esther 6:10). The humiliation this brought down on Haman was a grave foreboding of what lay ahead for him. His wife and his wise men were the ones to deliver the dark news: *"If Mordecai, before whom you have begun to fall, is of the Jewish people, you will not prevail against him but will surely fall before him"* (Esther 6:13).

Just as Haman heard these words, the king's servants arrived to take him to Esther's dinner party. While they were all drinking wine, the king asked Ester again for her petition of him. Esther knew that in the brief time since her previous dinner, Haman's position in the realm had radically changed. Her moment had finally arrived! In great humility and with profound clarity, she told the king of Haman's murderous plan to annihilate all her people, a plan he manipulated the king to support and decree. The king was furious to hear of it; he left the room to get fresh air in the palace garden, to clear his head. Haman was terrified, so he threw himself on Esther's couch to *"beg for his life from Queen Esther"* (Esther 7:7). Just at that moment, the king returned to see this sight. He assumed Haman was assaulting Esther, so he immediately pronounced a death sentence for him. The gallows Haman had built for Mordecai would be used to end his life, as the king said, *"'Hang him on that.' So they hanged Haman on the gallows which he had prepared for Mordecai. Then the anger of the king abated"* (Esther 7:10).

Although Haman was gone, the edict against the Jews that he promulgated was not. A royal edict could not be undone; there was no way to revoke it. Seeing this problem and knowing what it meant for her people, Esther stood before the king again to intercede for them. It was true that the king could not take back his earlier proclamation against the Jews, but he could issue another one, allowing them to take up arms to defend themselves whenever they were attacked. They would not become victims of hatred again. The king followed Esther's advice. He issued a second edict that granted her suggestion. This was cause for great rejoicing among the Jews living throughout the empire. Mordecai, who became the king's high official in place of

Haman, together with Queen Esther declared official days of annual feasting and merriment to celebrate God's miraculous deliverance of his people. It was called the festival of Purim or "lots." It remembers how Haman had chosen the day for the Jews' annihilation by casting lots, but, because they were able to arm themselves, when that day arrived their enemies were destroyed instead. Jews have celebrated this great reversal of "lots" down to our own day.

The book of Esther ends with Mordecai recalling a dream he described in its very first chapter (although numbered as "11" in some Bibles; see Esther 11:5–12). He had seen two fierce dragons facing each other as they prepared to fight. One dragon represented a *"righteous nation."* All the other nations who wanted to wage war against it were represented in the second dragon. The righteous nation cried out to God for help, *"and from their cry, as though from a tiny spring, there came a great river, with abundant water; light came, and the sun rose, and the lowly were exalted and consumed those held in honor."*

Mordecai saw his dream fulfilled. Esther was the *"tiny spring which became a river, and there was light and the sun and abundant water"* (Esther 10:6). We can see the story of all salvation history in Esther's story, as the Church teaches: "Against all human expectation God chooses those who were considered powerless and weak to show forth his faithfulness to his promises" (CCC 489). What a remarkable story it is!

Esther and Mary

Esther is the second woman of the Old Testament, after Bathsheba, to be elevated to the royal position of queen through unlikely circumstances. Both were devout and beautiful; both were taken away from the life they had perhaps imagined they would live by men who were enamored of their beauty. They both used their position as queens to advocate for those who needed their help. Both women figure prominently in the establishment of new and lasting traditions for God's people. Bathsheba was the first queen mother, the *gebirah*, of Israel, with her own throne at the right hand of the king. Thereafter, the queen of Israel would always be the king's mother, not his wife. Esther, along with Mordecai, presided over the creation of the festival of Purim for the Jews. Two days of feasting and merriment to celebrate their deliverance from their enemies were to be observed every year among them "*and kept throughout every generation ... that these days of Purim should never fall into disuse ... [or] cease among their descendants*" (Esther 9:28). These were two women who became queens without grasping their positions—one in Israel, the other in a pagan, Gentile empire— two advocates for people in need, two participants in new institutions in the life of God's people. Can we now add a third such queen?

We have already pondered how Bathsheba was a type of Mary; we should have no difficulty seeing that in Esther, too. In fact, when we consider Esther this way, we are standing on firm ground, verified by St. John Paul II:

> Esther did not kill the enemy, but by playing the role of mediator, interceded for those who were threatened by destruction ... The Old Testament tradition frequently emphasizes the decisive action of women in the salvation of Israel, especially in the writings closest to the coming of Christ [i.e., the book of Esther]. In this way the Holy Spirit,

through the events connected with Old Testament women, sketches with ever greater precision the characteristics of Mary's mission in the work of salvation for the entire human race.[36]

Beyond her work as mediator and intercessor for her people, Esther has more to commend her as a type of Mary. As described by Bishop F. Justus Knecht,

> Esther, on account of her beauty, was raised from her low estate to be queen; Mary, on account of her pure and humble heart, was raised to be the Mother of the Redeemer, and afterward, Queen of Heaven. Esther alone was exempted from the king's severe law; Mary alone is exempted from the curse of original sin. Esther, adorned in splendid garments, went before the king, prayed for her people, and was heard; Mary, the Queen of Heaven, radiant with virtues and merits, goes before the throne of God to intercede for her people.[37]

Esther, in her humble, faithful obedience to God, became the one through whom he worked great reversals for her and her people. Mary, in her humble, faithful obedience to God, became the one through whom he worked the greatest reversal in human history—our redemption. Esther's obedience led to the overthrow of Haman, the vicious, murderous enemy of the Jews. Mary's obedience led to the overthrow of Satan, the vicious, murderous enemy of all God's people. Esther's elevation to be queen led to a superabundance of goodness to others, gifts to them throughout the empire. Mary's elevation led to a superabundance of gifts to God's people, as we regularly proclaim: "Hail, Holy Queen, Mother of Mercy, our life, our sweetness, and our hope." Esther's freedom from the king's law of death came from her royal dignity, conferred on her by the king himself; her people came to share that freedom through her intercession. Mary's freedom from the law of sin and death came from God's kindness to her at her conception; we have come to share that freedom through her obedience in giving birth to Jesus, our Redeemer from sin and death.

Finally, some in our tradition have seen the festival of Purim as a type of the feast of Easter. St. Athanasius called his flock to have the same delight in their celebration of Easter as the Jews had when they celebrated Purim in Esther's time:

> Let us keep the feast in that way that he has established for our salvation—the holy day of Easter ... Remember that ... in the time of Esther the people kept a feast to the Lord because they had been delivered from a deadly decree. They called a feast, thanking and praising the Lord because he had changed the situation for them. Therefore, let us keep our promises to the Lord, confess our sins, and keep the feast to him—in behavior, moral conduct, and way of life.[38]

Esther and Mary were each a *"tiny spring which became a river, and there was light and the sun and abundant water."* Mordecai's dream has now been well and truly fulfilled.

— *Pondering Esther* —

Esther's is an almost unbelievable story of elevation from the life of a simple, obscure Jewish girl to be queen of Persia. She neither sought nor grasped at this elevation; it was thrust upon her. We know from her prayer that she did not want to be queen—not at all. Nevertheless, she bore herself in composure and peace; she maintained an inner calm that kept her outer appearance beautiful. Again, we saw from her prayer that in her difficult situation she found joy from her confidence that God was with her. However, before her heroic moment arrived, did she wonder why it had happened to her, why she could not go back to her uncle and the life they shared before? If so, Mordecai gave her the answer: God arranged it for his own purposes.

- There are times when we, too, can experience a radical change in our situation—perhaps an unpleasant one—that baffles us about how or why it happened. Sometimes these are simply circumstantial; some changes, unwanted, come to us through others. Esther knew that kind of change. Still, she was able to know the joy and steadiness in such circumstances that can come from God alone. She knew she was his beloved daughter, no matter what happened in her life.

- Are you in a time now when you need Esther's voice to speak to you? Can you be as honest as she was about what you need from God? In time, he made her difficult life fruitful. Can you believe that God can do for you what he did for her?

Esther prayed fervently about her difficult situation, and she was always entirely honest about the fear she experienced. She was able to do what she had to do, trusting in God's help, but her "*heart was frozen with fear*." Fear becomes an enemy only if it convinces us we cannot do what God asks of us. As Mother Agnes of Jesus, Carmelite nun and sister of St. Thérèse of Lisieux, wrote:

> "I opened the Gospel and read these words: *They were going up to Jerusalem and Jesus walked ahead of them, and his disciples followed him trembling* (Mk 10:32). Does not that happen to us sometimes; we follow Jesus trembling when we know he is leading us to Calvary? But we need not worry, we do not offend him by trembling; we would offend him only if we refused to follow him."[39]

Sometimes fear can be a friend, because it moves us to cry out to God for help, as Esther did. Even when he gives us the grace to obey, to do the difficult thing, the *feeling* of fear may remain.

- Do you ever struggle with fear when you see the path that God has set before you, or when complications multiply and mount up as you seek to follow it? Esther is an example of trusting God in situations like that. Many years after she lived, St. Paul would describe how to follow Jesus right through the fears that can beset us: "*Have no anxiety about anything, but in everything by prayer and supplication with thanksgiving let your requests be made known to God. And the peace of God, which passes all understanding, will keep your hearts and minds in Christ Jesus*" (Philippians 4:6–7).

- Is this encouragement, from both Esther and St. Paul, what your heart and mind need today?

Are there any lingering impressions from Esther's life that you do not want to forget? Perhaps you can write them down here or in your own journal.

....

....

....

....

....

....

....

....

....

Historical Note: The book of Esther belongs in the time period of the Return, although Esther lived in the land of exile, in Susa, the capital city of the Persians. King Ahasuerus ruled from 486-465 BC, after the Jewish people had begun to return to the Holy Land. The return of the Jews spanned many years, however. At the time of Esther's story, the Temple had been rebuilt, but the walls of Jerusalem had not yet been restored.

Chapter Ten

Judith—In the Time of
the Return

"O daughter, you are blessed by the Most High God
above all women on earth; and blessed be the Lord God
who ... has guided you to strike the head of the leader of
our enemies ... May God grant this to be a
perpetual honor to you."

—Judith 13:18, 20

Historical Context: Return (538–167 BC)

After enduring a long and purifying exile from the Holy Land, the
Jews were allowed to return to their homeland by a decree from
Cyrus, king of Persia, beginning in 538 BC. Cyrus even provided
money for the rebuilding of the Temple, which was thoroughly
destroyed when the Babylonians ravaged Jerusalem. When the
construction was begun, the older Jews who had seen the original
Temple built by Solomon wept in dismay; the new could not
compare with the glory of the old. Still, over time, the nation
of Judah was restored enough to have city walls built around
Jerusalem to protect it from invasion, a temple for liturgical
worship, and a renewed knowledge of the Torah, the first five
books of the Old Testament. However, there was no Davidic

king to sit on the throne and no Ark of the Covenant in the most sacred part of the temple, the Holy of Holies. The Ark, which God directed Moses to have made (see Exodus 25:10–22) had been lost during the Babylonian conquest. There were constant threats of foreign attacks and rule. It was truly a nation still waiting for all the promises of God to be realized, especially for a son of David to rule the kingdom once again, leading them to freedom and peace.

During this Return period we meet a woman named Judith. Hers is an unforgettable story, so full of drama that it would make a thrilling, captivating movie. Yet its spiritual value to us far exceeds anything we could get from the big screen.

Note: Scholars have recognized challenges in determining the historicity of the book of Judith because it contains several historical anomalies. For example, in Judith, it is said that Nebuchadnezzar reigns as king of Persia during the postexilic period, although we know with certainty he reigned over Babylon, not Persia, many years earlier. This comment from *A Catholic Introduction to the Bible: Old Testament* can be helpful:

> In light of such difficulties, it is unlikely that the book of Judith as we have it intends to be a strictly historical book. Two alternatives for the book's literary genre are either *cryptic historical* or *historical fiction*. If Judith is cryptic history, the names and characters of the book are ciphers for historical personages whom, for whatever reason, the author does not wish openly to identify, probably because the political situation at the time of writing was still too volatile. The other possibility is that Judith is intentional historical fiction or "historical romance." Against this theory, however, is the fact that the most ancient readers of

the text that we possess—the early Church Fathers—all seem to have regarded the book of Judith as a historical narrative and Judith as an actual historical figure.[40]

The Woman, Judith

The Jews who lived during the time of the Exile were chastened by the utter loss of their covenant identity. Without their land and the city beloved of David, Jerusalem, as well as their Temple, priests, and sacrifices, they had enough time and sorrow to recognize their national sins that brought down upon them God's just judgment. When they once again lived in the Holy Land and were able to practice covenant fidelity, they were determined to resist any pagan influences, especially those that came through alliances with pagan powers.

The temptation to form such alliances was frequent and strong, however. It was a turbulent time in the history of the world, when many pagan powers were on the march and empires were being established or overthrown. Armies were constantly preying on whatever town or village they could swallow up, extending the boundaries of their empires.

In Judith's story, the Assyrian army was poised to attack the hill town of Bethulia where Judith lived. It was a small town of seemingly no consequence, except that it was a gateway to Jerusalem and its Temple, the heart of Judah. Attacking Jerusalem was the real goal of the enemy army; conquering Bethulia would be its first step. The men of Bethulia stationed themselves in the hills to protect it. They were no match for the massive, well-equipped Assyrian army, but the topography of the land worked in their favor. The enemy would have to climb high hills to get anywhere near the town.

As the Assyrian king and his advisors discussed plans to defeat the town, a mercenary soldier named Achior, who was an Ammonite, had a word of warning for him. He had experience fighting against Israelites. He told the king that it was pointless to fight against them unless they disobeyed their God. If they kept God's law, they would always win (see Judith 5:20–21). The king ridiculed this idea and mocked Achior. As punishment for expressing doubt about his victory against Bethulia, he sent Achior, in the custody of his servants, to live with the Israelites so confident was he that Achior, along with all the Israelites, would die in the attack he planned.

The king commissioned a man named Holofernes to be commander of the forces that would take Bethulia. As the man responsible for the town's defeat, Holofernes decided the easiest way to victory was to cut off the town's sole water supply. That would be far cheaper than staging a full battle as it would spare the lives of many of his soldiers. So, Bethulia's water supply was completely shut off and panic followed.

In time, because there had been no rain, the situation in Bethulia became very desperate.

The people turned on their leaders, saying, *"You have done us a great injury in not making peace with the Assyrians. For now we have no one to help us; God has sold us into their hands, to strew us on the ground before them with thirst and utter destruction"* (Judith 7:24–25). They demanded that their leaders turn over their town to the Assyrians, giving up their freedom in exchange for their lives. The people assumed God had sold them into the hands of their enemies because of some infraction of his law, for that was how it was before the Exile. The irony was that they had not broken God's law, but if they surrendered to the pagan enemy rather than trusting him to save them, they would break this law. Uzziah, their governor, was hard-pressed, as we can imagine, so he proposed a compromise, postponing a decision for a few days but agreeing to surrender if no solution presented itself by the end of that time (see Judith 7:30–31).

It is here that Judith, whose name means "Jewish woman," enters the story. She was a young widow who had lived with her husband, Manasseh, for only three years before he died; they had no children. He left her a large estate, so she was very wealthy. She was also beautiful. Judith could have had a life very different from the one she chose: *"She set up a tent for herself on the roof of her house, and belted sackcloth about her loins, and wore the garments of her widowhood. She fasted all the days of her widowhood, except the day before the sabbath and the sabbath itself ... and the feasts and days of rejoicing of the house of Israel."* (Judith 8:5–6). Judith received stunning beauty by birth, but that was not all. *"She was beautiful in appearance, and had a very lovely face; she was prudent of heart, discerning in judgment, and quite virtuous ... No one spoke ill of her, for she feared God with great devotion"* (Judith 8:7–8). She had a *"very lovely face"* because of the goodness that resided in her through her ascetical life, in her great and serious devotion to God. We recall that Esther had this same quality of goodness that made her what Scripture calls *"lovely."* Judith's devout life was well-known throughout Bethulia. It would only be a matter of time before word got back to her of Uzziah's plan.

When she heard it, she was horrified. She gave the rulers a remarkable admonition:

> *"Who are you, that have put God to the test this day and are setting yourselves up in the place of God among the sons of men? ... No, my*

brethren, do not provoke the Lord our God to anger. For if he does not choose to help us within these five days, he has power to protect us within any time he pleases, or even to destroy us in the presence of our enemies. Do not try to bind the purposes of the Lord our God; for God is not like man, to be threatened, nor like a human being, to be won over by pleading. Therefore, while we wait for his deliverance, let us call upon him to help us, and he will hear our voice, if it pleases him." (Judith 8:12–17)

In this, we see that Judith had a profound understanding of the providence of God and the foolishness of trying to bind him to the plans of man. Hers was a deep expression of the attitude of obedience that Jesus and Mary, many centuries later, would both express in words: *"Not my will but yours be done"* (Luke 22:42) and *"Let it be to me according to your word"* (Luke 1:38). Judith urged the rulers to keep covenant with God, to put their trust in him alone and forget about their timetable. She believed the fate of the people, the safety of the Temple in Jerusalem, and their national identity depended on the town's faithfulness. She learned from the people's complaint to Uzziah that they believed the lack of rain and their terrible predicament were God's punishment for their sins and the sins of their fathers. Judith saw it differently: *"In spite of everything let us give thanks to the Lord our God, who is putting us to the test as he did our forefathers ... the Lord scourges those who draw near to him, in order to admonish them"* (Judith 8:25, 27; see also Hebrews 12:5–11). She told the rulers this was a test of faith, in the same way God tested Abraham, Isaac, and Jacob. She wanted them to be thankful for it. Uzziah recognized the wisdom of her words, yet he replied, *"The people were very thirsty, and they compelled us to do for them what we have promised, and made us take an oath which we cannot break."* (Judith 8:30).

As Uzziah acknowledged, Judith was a wise woman. She could see that all her pleading fell on deaf ears. Did the town rulers really believe that the oath they should never have sworn, the one that held within it the intention to break covenant with God, was binding on them? Or did they simply fear the angry wrath of the townspeople who might turn against them? In frustration with this shocking lack of leadership in the men appointed to it, Judith devised a plan of her own. She told the leaders, *"Stand at the city gate tonight, and I will go out with my maid; and within the days after which you have promised to surrender the city to our enemies, the Lord will deliver Israel by my hand"* (Judith 8:32–33).

Judith planned to trick the enemy commander, Holofernes, into believing that she was a traitor to her people. She would have to gain his trust, and she would use that trust as the occasion of his downfall. It would be a very dangerous operation; we can see why she kept it a secret from the men, who would undoubtedly try to prevent her from carrying it out. She boldly predicted success for her plan: *"the Lord will deliver Israel by my hand."* What did the rulers make of that? Perhaps it left them speechless; all they could do was wish her well.

Before she put her plan into action, *"Judith cried out to the Lord with a loud voice ... 'O God, my God, hear me ... a widow ... For your power depends not upon numbers, nor your might upon men of strength; for you are God of the lowly, helper of the oppressed, upholder of the weak, protector of the forlorn, savior of those without hope'"* (Judith 9:1, 4, 11). Judith understood that God's power did not depend on what appears powerful in this world—large armies and many men of great strength. God's power comes from himself—from his character, his goodness. He chooses those who, in the eyes of the world, are *"without hope"* to unleash it. When she joined her prayer to the evening sacrifice of incense in the Temple, Judith counted herself among that number.

After praying, Judith prepared to put her plan into action.

> [She] *bathed her body ... and arrayed herself in her most festive apparel, which she used to wear while her husband Manasseh was living. And she put sandals on her feet, and put on her anklets and bracelets and rings, and her earrings and all her ornaments, and made herself very beautiful, to entice the eyes of all men who might see her. And she gave her maid a bottle of wine and a flask of oil, and filled a bag with parched grain and a cake of dried fruit and fine bread; and she wrapped up all her vessels and gave them to her to carry.* (Judith 10:3–5)

This was quite a transformation! She dressed as she had done as a beautiful wife as she went into battle against Israel's enemy. She took with her food to eat while she and her maid were in the enemy camp so as not to defile themselves by eating ritually unclean pagan food. She carried wine, oil, and bread with her. These were significant elements in the life of pious Jews, as they would later become in our own lives, too.

Dressed in all her finery, Judith had a stunning effect on everyone who saw her, beginning with the elders of her own town, who blessed her (see Judith 10:7–8). The men who saw her did not lust after her. How do we know that? Seeing her beauty led them to ask for God's help for her *"that the people of Israel may glory and Jerusalem be exalted."* Seductive beauty in a woman does not do that. For her part, upon hearing what the men said, Judith *"worshiped God."* She would not have been able to do that if she had been the cause of lust.

Judith and her maid left for the enemy camp that night. They were captured, just as she had planned. She identified herself as a daughter of the Hebrews and described her mission: to tell Holofernes how he could win the battle with no losses to his side (see Judith 10:13). The enemy soldiers were also spellbound by Judith's beauty: *"When the men heard her words, and observed her face—she was in their eyes marvelously beautiful—they said to her ... 'Go at once to his tent; some of us will escort you and hand you over to him. And when you stand before him, do not be afraid in your heart, but tell him just what you have said, and he will treat you well'"* (Judith 10:14–16).

These soldiers, on the outskirts of the enemy camp, could have set upon the beautiful Judith and her maid for their own purposes. Who would have seen or known about it in the camp? Instead, we see the remarkable effect of Judith's *"marvelously beautiful"* appearance. Even in enemy soldiers, it led not to lust but to what seemed like goodness to them. These men were soldiers; their job was to fight for victory for their nation. Judith's plan seemed to serve that purpose, so they wanted her to succeed in her mission. The men offered her an escort and coached her on how to present her plan to Holofernes. They wanted her to be free from fear; they were sure that if she followed their advice, Holofernes would treat her well, and she would complete her mission. In fact, that is exactly what happened.

When Judith and her maid arrived in the enemy camp, there arose a buzz of excitement among the soldiers. Here, we continue to see the true power of Judith's beauty. The enemy soldiers *"marveled at her beauty, and admired the Israelites"* (Judith 10:19). They thought that if a woman like Judith represented the whole nation, surely they must be a people who could *"ensnare the whole world"* (Judith 10:19). Simply looking at Judith, beholding her *"lovely face"* (Judith 8:7), inspired awe of God's people in enemy hearts. Can there be feminine beauty more powerful than that?

When her escort delivered her to their commander's tent, Holofernes came out to meet her and was struck by her beauty (Judith 10:23). It was time for Judith to set her plan in motion. Seeing the awe her beauty inspired on the faces of Holofernes and his servants, she quickly struck a posture of humility before him. By this, she convinced him she was ready to serve and help him in his fight against the Israelites.

Holofernes asked her about her plan, with assurances that she was safe with him—no need to fear. Judith explained that the reason she knew he and his forces could defeat her people was because they were about to sin against their God. Recall that Achior, the Ammonite, had been ridiculed and sent away from the king for trying to warn him of this truth. Judith hid the real reason for the town's potential sin—they planned to surrender to the Assyrians and submit to them as rulers, a rebellious expression of covenant infidelity. Instead, she told Holofernes the people were in such desperation from lack of water they were about to eat and drink unclean food forbidden by God's law. She assured him that on the day they decided to act on this disobedient plan, they were doomed.

Through the years, questions have arisen about Judith's deception here. She lied, and that suggests to some that sometimes lies are not wrong if they serve a good end. In that historical time, deception was considered a valid weapon of war. We recall that Rahab lied to the king's men who sought the Israelite spies in her inn. The Fathers of the Church, considering this question, explained that in the economy of salvation, it took time for God to reveal the fullness of morality to his people. That fullness was not complete until Jesus came into human history. When he returned to heaven, the Church he established by Peter and the Apostles was given the charism of interpreting that fullness to God's people. Now we know that it is never right to lie; the end does not justify the means. Judith's virtue, they said, can be praised because her actions were all ordered to God's glory and the salvation of his people, not to personal gain or glory. We do not praise the deception.

After Judith told Holofernes why she knew her people would fall into his hands, she explained her role in that fall. She had left her people, she said, because of her devotion; she would not remain with them in their sin. Now, she declared, she would stay with Holofernes but would pray nightly outside the camp, and when she found out in prayer that the time was right for Holofernes to attack, she would pass that information along to him. In that way he would be assured of victory.

Judith and her maid set up their own tent in the camp. They were there during the day, but at night they were allowed to go outside the camp to pray and discern the time of the attack. They always ate only the food in their own bag, enabling them to refuse any unclean food offered by the soldiers. By praying every night and adhering strictly to their dietary laws, Judith was able to convince Holofernes that she was *"religious"* (Judith 11:16) and would be able to perceive the right time to attack as she claimed.

This went on for three days; on the fourth day, Holofernes held a banquet with only his servants in attendance. He invited Judith to join him, and she accepted: *"So she got up and arrayed herself in all her woman's finery ... and Holofernes' heart was ravished with her and he was moved with great desire to possess her; for he had been waiting for an opportunity to deceive her, ever since the day he first saw her"* (Judith 12:15–16). Now, we see what was in Holofernes' heart—lust and deception—from the start. His reaction to her beauty, unlike all the other men who beheld it, was evil. His words of comfort and assurance on the day he first saw her (see Judith 11:1–4) were lies. There is here the hissing sound of the Serpent in the Garden, whispering deceit into Eve's ear. Judith, however, was not taken in by it. The irony is that Holofernes thought he had deceived her into his tent to gain possession of her. He did not know that Judith had deceived him into his loss not only of her body but of his own, as well.

Holofernes wined and dined Judith, then he sent out all his servants. He and Judith were finally alone. He made himself merry with wine and, perhaps with Judith's encouragement, he drank too much. Excessive self-indulgence, as we know, can stupefy. Holofernes, the mighty warrior, could not escape the wine's numbing spell; he fell sound asleep. Judith recognized her heroic moment and prayed, *"O Lord God of all might, look in this hour upon the work of my hands for the exaltation of Jerusalem. For now is the time to help your inheritance, and to carry out my undertaking for the destruction of the enemies who have risen up against us"* (Judith 13:4–5). While her maid waited outside the tent, Judith took the sword of Holofernes and beheaded him (see Judith 13:8). By his own hand, Holofernes put himself to sleep in the presence of his enemy; by her own hand, Judith, awake to her need for God's help, gained the victory over him.

She left the tent with Holofernes' head, which she and her maid put in their food bag. They went out and did what they had done every night when they left the camp to pray, thus arousing no suspicion. They simply kept going until they reached the city gate of Bethulia. Filled with the excitement of her success, Judith *"called out from afar to the watchmen at the gates, 'Open, open the gate! God, our God, is still with us, to show his power in Israel, and his strength against our enemies, even as he has done this day!"* (Judith 13:11).

When her voice, echoing through the thin night air, fell on the ears of the elders within the city, they rushed down to the gate to let Judith and her maid enter. They could scarcely believe she had returned already from her dangerous mission. As they stood around a fire, she told them all that had happened: *"See, here is the head of Holofernes ... The Lord has struck him down by the hand of a woman. As the Lord lives, who has protected me in the way I went, it was my face that tricked him to his destruction, and yet he committed no act of sin with me, to defile and shame me"* (Judith 13:15–16). Judith understood that from beginning to end, the Lord had cared for her in every way, not only in enabling her to destroy the enemy *"by the hand of a woman"* but also preserving her in what mattered most. Although her beauty *"tricked* [Holofernes] *to his destruction,"* she was able to remain true to the source of that beauty, her own devotion to God. Her face had led others to whatever goodness was in them; for Holofernes, her face of pure goodness unmasked his face of pure evil, yet his evil did not *"defile or shame"* her.

When the elders heard her story, they *"were greatly astonished, and bowed down and worshiped God"* (Judith 13:17). Uzziah, who had earlier been unwilling to heed Judith's warning, acknowledged what had become crystal clear:

> *"O daughter, you are blessed by the Most High God above all women on earth; and blessed be the Lord God, who ... has guided you to strike the head of the leader of our enemies ... May God*

grant this to be a perpetual honor to you ... because you did not spare your own life when our nation was brought low, ... walking in the straight path before our God" (Judith 13:18, 20).

Although the elders wanted to praise Judith for what she had done, her mind was elsewhere. This was, after all, a true battle; there was still physical fighting that had to be done. Judith removed the enemy leader; the fighting men of Israel had to take advantage of her victory with their own faith and courage. She urged them to make haste to attack the Assyrians. Without their leader, many soldiers would flee; the enemy could quickly be driven away. They took her advice this time. They chased the Assyrians far from them and were able to live in peace again. Because Jerusalem, too, had been saved by Judith's bravery, the whole town of Bethulia traveled to Jerusalem for a lengthy celebration, and the high priest blessed Judith for her faith and courage: *"You are the exaltation of Jerusalem, you are the great glory of Israel, you are the great pride of our nation! You have done all this singlehanded; you have done great good to Israel, and God is well pleased with it. May the Almighty Lord bless you forever!"* (Judith 15:9–10). This is a remarkable priestly blessing on a woman; it recognized her singular role in saving her people. Without Judith's action, Israel would have been lost.

Instead of destruction by the hand of an enemy, there was great jubilation in Israel over their victory by the hand of a woman: *"Then all the women of Israel gathered to see her, and blessed her, and some of them performed a dance for her ... and she went before all the people in the dance, leading all the women, while all the men of Israel followed, bearing their arms and wearing garlands and with songs on their lips"* (Judith 15:12–13). This scene is reminiscent of Israel's great jubilation at the shore of the Red Sea after their deliverance from Pharoah and his armies, when Moses and Miriam led the people in singing God's praises (see Exodus 15:1–21). Then, as Miriam had done long before her, Judith led the people in song: *"Begin a song to my God with tambourines ... the Lord Almighty has foiled them* [the enemy] *by the hand of a woman ... with the beauty of her countenance"* (Judith 16:2, 6–7).

We recall that when Judith first urged the elders of the town to put their trust in God alone, no matter what the consequences, we recognized her deep understanding of God's providence. In her song, she once again expressed a great truth that her people often struggled to grasp: *"I will sing to my God a new song: O Lord, you are great and glorious, wonderful in strength, invincible ... to those who fear you you will continue to show mercy. For every sacrifice as a fragrant offering is a small thing, and all fat for burnt offerings to you is a very little thing, but he who fears the Lord shall be great for ever"* (Judith 16:13, 15–16). Judith knew that an outward show of liturgical correctness was a *"very little thing."* The Lord was looking for those who truly feared and trusted him, as she did. She knew that her greatness, proclaimed by all the people, lay there.

After this festive celebration in Jerusalem, Judith returned to her simple, small life in Bethulia. Although her fame spread far and wide, she turned down many suitors who sought her out, preferring to remain a widow. She freed her maid and gave away all her possessions before she died at the age of one hundred and five years (see Judith 16:21–25). Her impact was long-lasting in the land: *"And no one ever again spread terror among the people of Israel in the days of Judith, or for a long time after her death"* (Judith 16:25).

Judith's story ends in spectacular fame, but we must not forget that it began in years of a quiet, intentionally simple, ascetical (self-denying) life on the roof of her house. She prayed, she fasted, she gave her body, mind, and heart, to God alone. Those hidden years prepared her to speak the truth when it was needed, to recognize the danger when the truth was rejected, and to offer herself to God to prevent the disaster that rejection was sure to bring. Courageous faith like Judith's does not happen overnight, without costing anything. Living with and for God the way she did gave her an unshakeable confidence in God's character. He could be trusted to keep covenant with his people, if only they would keep covenant with him. She had no fear for her life; her only concern was for the glory of God and the deliverance of his people. She was able to step into her heroic moment and, when it was fulfilled, step back into her quiet, pious widowhood.

Judith's luminous life has been praised since the earliest days of the Church. In one of the oldest extra-biblical Christian writings we have, the first letter of St. Clement, Bishop of Rome, to the Corinthians, we read: "Many women ... being strengthened by the grace of God have performed numerous manly exploits ... Judith ... exposing herself to danger ... went out for the love which she bare to her country and people ... and the Lord delivered Holofernes into the hands of a woman."[41]

This description of Judith evokes the promise of God in the Garden after the Fall: "*I will put enmity between you and the woman, and between your seed and her seed*" (Genesis 3:15). The Garden of Eden is exactly where we want to be now as we think about the woman God promised there and the woman, Judith, who, indeed, "performed many manly exploits."

Judith and Mary

Judith is the first Old Testament woman we have met who planned to face a powerful, dreaded enemy commander and his legion of soldiers with confidence in her victory over them. We have seen women who were close to battles but not as we see Judith. Recall that Miriam and all God's people were able to escape a battle with Pharoah and his forces through God's miraculous deliverance at the Red Sea. Rahab remained safe in her home while a battle raged around her in Jericho. Deborah went into battle reluctantly with Barak, but only as his assistant; she did not take up arms. Jael was able to destroy Israel's enemy when he showed up unexpectedly at her tent. She took advantage of her heroic moment without laying a plan for it. Judith, however, went right to the heart of danger and by her own hand delivered her people from the evil Holofernes. Her role was pivotal but not solitary. She knew that the Israelite soldiers still had to fight a battle to defend Bethulia. Together, their defeat of the enemy gave their people peace and rest for a long time to come. So, why does Judith's life, especially her defeat of the enemy commander by lopping off his head, put us in mind of the Garden of Eden?

At the time of the Fall, God's first action to redeem his people from its effect was to tell the Serpent his destiny. A woman and her son would take up this battle, begun there in the Garden, and finish it. The Serpent's head would be wounded—crushed. The woman and her son would know pain, but it would not be the end of them. All creation then began its long wait for the arrival of that woman, the mother-warrior, and her son, the victor, in their great and final battle for the deliverance of mankind from the evil unleashed in the Garden.

In Judith, we find a woman unique in the Old Testament. Her devout, ascetical life, her beauty and loveliness, her faith and courage, and her brave willingness to face pure evil head-on commend her to us as a type of Mary *par excellence*. Although Judith's battle against the enemy was physical, played out within the historical realities of her time, she always saw its spiritual nature. To Judith, the Assyrian threat was the threat of evil against God's goodness. It was cosmic in nature, even as it was fought by soldiers with swords, in the dust of the earth, with blood on the ground. Her story deepens our understanding and expectation of the mother-warrior yet to come. That woman would be a pure, devout woman, aware of her lowliness, who would recognize her heroic moment and give herself completely to it. Her role in God's plan to conquer his enemy would be pivotal but not solitary. She and her son, together, would end the tyranny of evil over God's good ("lovely," in Hebrew) creation forever.

We see so many hints of Mary's life in Judith's story. As Bishop Knecht writes,

> Even as chaste Judith cut off the head of Holofernes, thereby saving her people from captivity and slavery, so did Mary, the Immaculate Mother through her Divine Son, trample on the head of the infernal Holofernes and free all mankind from his power. Even as Judith was lauded as 'blessed above all women on earth,' so did St. Elizabeth and the angel, Gabriel, both say to our Lady: 'Blessed art thou among women.' Judith gave all glory to God, as did Mary in her *Magnificat* ... Judith was heroic: Mary was the most heroic of women, who also risked death [by stoning for adultery] to become mother of the Messiah. Judith was the glory of Jerusalem: Mary is the Queen of all saints, the glory of the heavenly Jerusalem, the joy of the elect, and the honor of the whole Church.[42]

— Pondering Judith —

Judith's story, so rich in details, especially in the number and length of her recorded prayers, offers us a feast of lessons on living a godly life, as she did. We have space here to consider only a few.

Judith's heroic life began on the roof of her house. She lived her days in extraordinary self-renunciation, the exact opposite of what often comes to mind when we think of heroics. She did not plan to live a grand life. In fact, she considered herself to be among the "*lowly*" of the earth, ever dependent on God for everything. Recall her prayer: "*O God, my God, hear me also, a widow … For your power depends not upon numbers, nor … upon men of strength; for you are God of the lowly, helper of the oppressed, upholder of the weak, protector of the forlorn, savior of those without hope*" (Judith 9:4, 11). Hers was a life of unrelenting yearning for God, expressed in fasting, prayer, and simplicity. Her self-discipline kept her alert to God; it enabled her to recognize her heroic moment when it arrived and step into it, for his glory, not her own.

Not many of us will be able to live Judith's rooftop renunciation of the world and of herself. Probably all of us, however, admire her great hunger for God and all the fruit that hunger produced in her.

- Can her example help us today to think about how we can better nurture our own hunger for God? What distractions might we need to give up? What might we need to add to our daily lives to better include him in our routine activities, both large and small?

Judith had a remarkable understanding of the providence of God. She urged the town elders to put all their trust in him for his help in their crisis. She knew this kind of trust was at the heart of being his covenant people. They needed to be so confident of his goodness that they would be willing to let him do whatever he wanted to do with them without fear, "*even to destroy us in the presence of our enemies*" (Judith 8:15). This is a statement of absolute confidence in God's wisdom, a rock-solid belief that he knows what we need and he knows what he is doing.

- Can we examine ourselves to see if Judith's confidence lives in us? Are we willing to go as far as she did in putting ourselves, our circumstances, our loved ones entirely in God's care? Jesus urged this confidence upon his disciples, too: "*In the world you have tribulation; but be of good cheer, I have overcome the world*" (John 16:33). Can his words help you trust him?

Judith's beauty was a powerful weapon in her battle against the enemy. Others who observed it were moved to goodness, too. When Holofernes saw her face, it so captivated him that it unmasked his evil heart. There was no goodness at all in him. Most of us are drawn to physical beauty, aren't we? When we see in Scripture a connection between beauty and goodness, as we did in Esther and Judith, we wonder about how this appeared in Mary, a woman *full* of grace, full of God's own goodness. How beautiful was she because of the goodness God gave her?

Judith's beauty came from inside; hers was a beautiful soul. In the New Testament, St. Peter wrote to Christian women about this kind of beauty: "*Let not yours be the outward adorning with braiding of hair, decoration of gold, and wearing of robes, but let it be the hidden person of the heart with the imperishable jewel of a gentle and quiet spirit, which in God's sight is very precious. So once the holy women who hoped in God used to adorn themselves*" (1 Peter 3:3–5).

- Can these words be a corrective for us away from mistaking glamour, style, or physical attractiveness for the beauty that pleases God? Can they help us preserve the proper balance between our natural and necessary attention to physical appearance and the attention we give to the "*hidden person of the heart*"? Can we work to cultivate in ourselves a "*gentle and quiet spirit*" in this noisy, frenetic world? Can "*the holy women who hoped in God*," from Eve to Judith, serve as examples to us in this?

After accomplishing her mission, Judith returned to her simple life in Bethulia. Even though her reputation spread far and wide, she attended to the routines that had grounded her so well in her devotion to God. In this, we see Judith's abiding *humility*, perhaps her outstanding virtue. She understood that her great victory over the enemy was for God's glory, not her own. She had received her mission from him; when it was completed, she did not grasp for more.

- What does it take for a woman of such accomplishment and reputation to step out of the limelight and return to smallness? Have you ever had a heroic moment that put

your name on people's lips? If so, what temptations came
with that? How well did you face them?

Are there any lingering impressions from Judith's life that you
do not want to forget? Perhaps you can write them down
here or in your own journal.

....

....

....

....

....

....

....

....

....

....

....

Chapter Eleven

The Mother of Martyrs—
In the Time of the
Maccabean Revolt

"My son ... I carried you nine months in my womb, and
nursed you for three years, and have reared you and brought
you up to this point in your life, and have taken care of you ...
Accept death, so that in God's mercy I may
get you back again."

—2 Maccabees 7:27, 29

Historical Context: Maccabean Revolt (167 BC–AD 1)

After the conquest of Judah's enemies by Judith and the men
of Bethulia, there was a period of peace and stability for their
nation, but it was only temporary. Eventually, in 333 BC, the
Greeks under the powerful direction of Alexander the Great
established control over the empire that had belonged to
the Persians. When Alexander died in his prime, leaving no
successor to his throne, the empire was split among his leading
generals. Initially, the Jews in Judah were ruled by Ptolemy,
who reigned in Egypt without much interference in the Jewish
way of life. However, when the rival Seleucid king conquered

the Ptolemies, taking control of the Holy Land, everything changed.

In 167 BC, Antiochus Epiphanes, whose name meant "God Manifest," aggressively attempted to replace Jewish religion and culture with Greek ideas and practices. His rule became a horrific time of suppression of God's covenant people. He desecrated the Temple in Jerusalem and required the Jews to betray the one true God by worshipping pagan gods, eating ritually unclean foods, and ceasing the rite of circumcision, the foundational sign of Jewish identity. Some Jews, attracted by the cosmopolitan and enlightened Greek culture, accepted these corruptions of Jewish life. They were ready to appease the Greeks in the hope of the political and social stability it seemed to provide.

Other Jews did not give in to this suppression, eventually taking up arms against the Greeks. They were led by a man named Mattathias and his sons, who became known as the Maccabees. In an unlikely victory, they managed to defeat their enemy, reclaiming control over their land, the Temple, and Jewish religion. That is why this time period is called the Maccabean Revolt. When they restored and purified the Temple from all the abominations that had taken place there, they celebrated with the feast called Hannukah, *"the feast of the Dedication,"* observed by Jesus (see John 10:22) and in our own day, as well.

The nation enjoyed a brief time of independence, lasting only about one hundred years. It ended with the Roman conquest of the Holy Land in 63 BC. Then Judah fell under Herodian rule that began with Herod the Great in 36 BC, a usurper king, not of David's line but supported by the Roman emperor. The Jewish people were under the rule of Herod the Great's sons when the long-awaited Messiah, Jesus, was born.

The history of this period is recorded in the first book of Maccabees; the second book of Maccabees recounts some of it but with a dramatic difference. Within its chapters that describe the vicious rule of Antiochus Epiphanes is the account of an alternative Jewish response to foreign domination. Some Jews willingly chose martyrdom for the sake of fidelity to God's covenant rather than obey the new anti-Jewish rules of their tyrant king. Among the martyrs was a mother whose faith and bravery stand out amid all that we have yet seen of the women of the Old Testament. We never learn her name. However, her story tells us much more about her than a name could possibly convey. She was the last great heroine of God's people before Gabriel's visit to Mary in Nazareth, less than two hundred years later. Her life is the final tile in the colorful, beautiful mosaic of Mary that has taken shape through the faith and courage of so many of the Old Testament heroines. Without this mother's story, the mosaic would not be complete.

The Woman, Mother of Martyrs

The two books of Maccabees tell us the history of how the Greeks intended to suppress Judaism completely. They tore down and tried to destroy what was sacred to the Jews as God's covenant people, replacing it with Greek pagan religion and ideals. The means they used to accomplish this were terrifying, especially to us as modern readers. The Jews who lived through it were shocked, too, by its cruelty. The author of the second book of Maccabees (unknown to us) felt the weight of the history he recorded. He expressed this in a rare "aside" in his account, directly addressing his readers:

Now I urge those who read this book not to be depressed by such calamities, but to recognize that these punishments were designed not to destroy but to discipline our people. In fact, not to let the impious alone for long, but to punish them immediately, is a sign of great kindness. For in the case of the other nations the Lord waits patiently to punish them until they have reached the full measure of their sins; but he does not deal in this way with us, in order that he may not take vengeance on us afterward when our sins have reached their height. Therefore he never withdraws his mercy from us. Though he disciplines us with calamities, he does not forsake his own people. (2 Maccabees 6:12–17)

This explanation is particularly fitting preparation for the dramatic, gruesome stories that follow.

First, there is an account of the elderly Eleazar, a respected man among the Jews. The Greek oppressors demanded that he violate the dietary laws God had given to the Jews (see 2 Maccabees 6:18). He manfully resisted all pressure to obey, even up to the point of death. *"When he was about to die under the blows* [of his torture], *he groaned aloud and said: 'It is clear to the Lord in his holy knowledge that, though I might have been saved from death, I am enduring terrible sufferings in my body under this beating, but in my soul I am glad to suffer these things because I fear him'"* (2 Maccabees 6:30). By his death, he set a noble, memorable example of courage for the sake of God's law to the whole nation.

The Greek rulers then turned their wrath, *"with whips and cords,"* against *"seven brothers and their mother,"* likewise pressuring them to eat the unlawful meat (2 Maccabees 7:1). One of the brothers told their persecutors that their torture was useless: *"We are ready to die rather than transgress the laws of our fathers"* (2 Maccabees 7:2). This resistance provoked the king into such a rage that he ordered unthinkable punishment for him. His tongue was cut out, his scalp removed, and his hands and feet were amputated, *"while the rest of the brothers and the mother looked on"* (2 Maccabees 7:4). As if that were not enough, while he was *"still breathing,"* he was thrown into a pan and fried (2 Maccabees 7:5). As electrified by this horror as his mother and brothers undoubtedly were, they encouraged one another to die nobly: *"The Lord God is watching over us and in truth has compassion on us, as Moses declared in his song which bore witness against the people to their faces, when he said, 'And he will have compassion on his servants'"* (2 Maccabees 7:6).

The torturers then turned on the next young man, who suffered the same fate as his brother. With his last breath, he spoke to his persecutors: *"You dismiss us from this present life, but the King of the universe will raise us up to an everlasting renewal of life, because we have died for his laws"* (2 Maccabees 7:9). The third brother went willingly to his death as well, boldly stretching out his hands for amputation with this announcement: *"I got these from Heaven, and because of his laws I disdain them, and from him I hope to get them back again"* (2 Maccabees 7:11). The young man's bravery astonished the king and the executioners, *"for he regarded his sufferings as nothing"* (2 Maccabees 7:12). The fourth brother was next in line. With his dying breath, he confirmed his confidence in his resurrection by God and warned his tormentors: *"But for you there will be no resurrection to life!"* (2 Maccabees 7:14).

The fifth brother, before his death, had strength enough to taunt the king: *"Do not think that God has forsaken our people. Keep on, and see how his mighty power will torture you and your descendants!"* (2 Maccabees 7:16–17). He was followed by the sixth brother, who regarded the suffering of all the brothers as just punishment on their own sins. He, too, warned the king of God's just punishments (see 2 Maccabees 7:18–19).

As agony after agony was heaped on this family, two questions arise. First, how were these young men able to face down torture and death with such strong faith and courage? Next, we must wonder how the mother could stand by and watch. Even to think about the mother's pain can cause us to shudder; it must have been excruciating. Who were these people? Who was this mother? To answer both these questions, we must now turn to her.

"The mother was especially admirable and worthy of honorable memory. Though she saw her seven sons perish within a single day, she bore it with good courage because of her hope in the Lord" (2 Maccabees 7:20). To watch her sons suffer as they did must have fallen on her as a crushing weight, a heaviness that surely would have taken her breath away, but she *"bore it with good courage."* It was as if her suffering was laid upon her back and meant to break it, but she did not break. What kept her strong? It was *"her hope in the Lord."* She found strength not only to stand and watch but also to encourage her sons:

> *She encouraged each of them in the language of their fathers. Filled with a noble spirit, she fired her woman's reasoning with a man's courage, and said to them, "I do not know how you came into being in my womb. It was not I who gave you life and breath, nor I who set in order the elements within each of you. Therefore the Creator of the world, who shaped the beginning of man and devised the origin of all things, will in his mercy give life and breath back to you again, since you now forget yourselves for the sake of his laws."* (2 Maccabees 7:21–23)

This noble mother *"fired her woman's reasoning with a man's courage."* What was her *"woman's reasoning"*? How is it unique, different from a man's reasoning? The mother, herself, explained it. A mother knows she did not create the *"life and breath"* of a child who takes shape within her womb. A mother, therefore, is closest to the deepest mystery of our existence: the formation of a human being by the Creator of the world. A father can imagine it; a mother experiences it in her own body. A *"woman's reasoning"* begins here. If the *"Creator of the world"* can do such a miraculous thing, he can do anything. Faith, then, is not a leap in the dark for a mother. No, for a mother, faith is a reasoned step from what is undeniably true from her own experience—God can work miracles for us—to concrete belief that he will have *"mercy"* on the creatures he brought into existence by his own will and for his own pleasure. The mother was confident that although her sons died for their love of God, he would *"in his mercy give life and breath back to* [them] *again."*

If we wonder how the young martyrs were able to welcome death for the love of God, we need only think about the mother who raised them. She must have nurtured them with the wisdom she once again whispered as they were dying. When they were growing from childhood to manhood, her boundless confidence in the goodness of God, the God who had formed them in her body, must have infused in them the confidence they themselves would need in their hour of trial. The faith they learned from their mother did not fail them.

Why did the mother need *"a man's courage"* to endure her suffering in such a noble way? What is unique about a man's courage, making it different from that of a woman? Watching the vicious king, in his next actions, will help us answer this question.

Antiochus, the king, *"was suspicious"* of the mother because of *"her reproachful tone"* (2 Maccabees 7:24). He decided to change his tactic with the youngest brother, the last one still alive, offering him wealth and honors if he would abandon his religion. The young man resisted the king's offer. Surprisingly, the king urged the mother *"to advise the youth to save himself"* (2 Maccabees 7:25). We know the king was suspicious of her, so why did he turn to her for help? He must have assumed that this tortured mother, who had only one young son left, would be overwhelmed by her powerful maternal emotion. He counted on the mysterious bond all mothers have with their children, thinking it would weaken the mother's resistance and drive her to prevent her son's death at all costs. Even this wicked king understood that women have a natural tenderness and concern for the weak, the helpless, the needy—a tenderness that can move them to pity. Women have a strong sense of what it is to be dependent on the help and care of others. The disparity of physical strength between men and woman means that every woman, at some point in her life, will likely need to depend on the help of the stronger sex for something. For women during their childbearing years, this is a frequent reality. The time and energy a mother must devote to caring for children means she must depend on her husband to care for her. Men are not usually drawn to weakness or helplessness in the same way as women. The differences between men and women, designed by God, always serve a purpose. They are not accidental or meaningless. Women's sensitivity to the hurting, the helpless, the lowly of the world is God's great gift to humanity.

Antiochus expected that the mother's emotional attachment to her last living son would finally move her to let go of her principles and do whatever it took to save him. He understood every mother's protective impulse to shield her child from suffering. However, the mother *"fired her woman's reasoning with a man's courage"* and put her powerful emotions aside. Men are regularly able to overcome emotion for the sake of what must be done, especially when what is required of them is difficult, frightening, or dangerous. This, too, is a great gift from God to us all. The mother thwarted the king by combining her woman's reasoning that God can be trusted to work miracles with a man's courage to act despite her emotions. She leaned close to her son and spoke in their native tongue. Her first words might surprise us: *"My son, have pity on me"* (2 Maccabees 7:27). It was he who was about to be tortured to death. Isn't it more reasonable that she would have pity on him?

The mother continued:

> *"I carried you nine months in my womb, and nursed you for three years, and have reared you and brought you up to this point in your life, and have taken care of you. I beg you, my child, to look at the heaven and the earth and see everything that is in them, and recognize that God did not make them out of things that existed. Thus also mankind comes into being. Do not fear this butcher, but prove worthy of your brothers. Accept death, so that in God's mercy I may get you back again with your brothers."* (2 Maccabees 7:27–29)

The mother asked the son's pity because she wanted him to remember the care she had given him all his life, from his conception in her womb to the moment of his impending death. All her nurturing served one purpose—that her son would grow up to know that his life was entirely in God's merciful hands.

She did not want to see her son forsake all that she worked hard to give him; his pity would spare her that. The mother's counsel urged her son to look at creation all around him, *"the heaven and the earth,"* to see evidence of God's power. Considering all that their eyes had seen that day in the brutal mutilation and extermination of their entire family, this is stunning advice. She wanted her son to look beyond the blood and gore to behold the beauty built into the universe by the God to whom everything belonged. The mother understood that this life is transitory. It is the eternal life with God, the one in which the dead receive each other back again alive forever, that matters.

The mother's wise words ignited a flame in her son. *"While she was still speaking, the young man said, 'What are you waiting for? I will not obey the king's command, but I obey the command of the law that was given to our fathers through Moses'"* (2 Maccabees 7:30). The mother's rich deposit of faith, given to her son all his life, bore fruit to make her proud. Her young son understood what was happening to him in a way that went far beyond his years:

> *"For our brothers after enduring a brief suffering have drunk of everflowing life under God's covenant; but you, by the judgment of God, will receive just punishment for your arrogance. I, like my brothers, give up body and life for the laws of our fathers, appealing to God to show mercy soon to our nation and by afflictions and plagues to make you confess that he alone is God, and through me and my brothers to bring to an end the wrath of the Almighty which has justly fallen on our whole nation."* (2 Maccabees 7:36–38)

He grasped a profound knowledge of the redemptive nature of this family's suffering. They were willing to die in the hope of ending *"the wrath of the Almighty which has justly fallen on our whole nation."* They believed the Greek conquest of their homeland and its people happened because of the Jews' indifference to their covenant life with God and the willingness of some Jews to capitulate to the pagan ways of the Greeks. If they offered their lives to expiate those national sins, they hoped God would free the Jews from foreign tyranny. With this reliance on God, the last son accepted torture. Then the mother was executed, as well (see 2 Maccabees 7:39–41).

Was the martyrs' hope of redemption for their nation fulfilled? Or did they die in vain, comforted briefly by a pious dream that had no substance to it? We must recall that the story of the martyrs was inserted into the retelling of the Maccabean revolt in the second book of Maccabees. Before it came a description of Judas Maccabeus and his sons withdrawing to the wilderness to remove themselves from pagan influence. After it comes the story of the improbably successful revolt Judas and his followers launched against the Greeks: *"The Gentiles could not withstand him* [Judas Maccabeus], *for the wrath of the Lord had turned to mercy"* (2 Maccabees 8:5). As Tim Gray and Jeff Cavins have noted: "If the Maccabean Revolt was successful, 2 Maccabees informs us, it was successful because of the martyrs, who by their fidelity and sacrifice had caused the wrath of the Lord to turn to mercy."[43]

The brave mother and her seven sons were not victims of a pie-in-the-sky fantasy. On the contrary, they give us a clear, riveting preview of another mother and son who would take up their hope of redemptive bloodshed and save the whole world in fulfilling it.

The Mother of Martyrs and Mary

What is unique about this mother among all the Old Testament women we have met and pondered here?

We have seen many other faithful, courageous women. Some gave birth to children miraculously. Some were great leaders who stepped into heroic moments given to them by God. Two were queens; one was a prostitute. Some were wealthy; one was desperately poor. Some were beautiful; all were humble. Yet none of them suffered as this mother did, who watched her seven sons die horrible deaths for love of God and his people. This apparently widowed mother (no husband is ever mentioned), in our brief encounter with her in Scripture, gives us a foreshadowing of what the mission of the Messiah's mother would include. Even though all the events recorded for us took place *"within a single day"* (2 Maccabees 7:20), our extended experience of her suffering, drawn out and prolonged by the graphic details of torture and death, hold us next to this mother, forcing us to endure what she saw, how she felt, what she did and did not do. We are not able to turn our gaze away from the horror of that day, a day that must have felt endless. Yet, consider this: If we were able to escape seeing and feeling what repels us, would we not also be shutting ourselves off from what is noble, magnificent, and of great value to our souls? If we do not run away from this scene, it will serve as our final preparation to meet Mary, the mother of the Messiah, and to understand her mission more deeply, perhaps, than we ever have before.

The mother of the Maccabees, by her wisdom and encouragement, helped her sons willingly accept their fates. She raised them from birth to know, love, and trust God with their lives. Her experience of receiving from God their bodies in her womb gave her assurance that he would not abandon them. She stayed steady as they died; her excruciating suffering was sevenfold. In this, Bishop Knecht says, her virtue exceeded that of her noble sons:

> She had the most to suffer, for in her heart she suffered all her sons' tortures. She was, in fact, an eightfold martyr, for she shared in the sufferings of each of her sons, and finally offered up her own life. In truth, the courage of the most valiant of soldiers cannot be compared with the heroism of this woman![44]

Within two hundred years of this dark day that the mother of the Maccabees suffered, Mary, the mother of the Messiah, lived through the day we call "Good Friday," when even the sun hid its face from that day's horror. As Gray and Cavins have written:

> It is not hard to imagine that during the events of Good Friday, Mary might have often recalled the noble spirit of the woman from 2 Maccabees 7, whose heart was broken having to watch the cruel torture and death suffered by her seven sons—but who was still able to encourage her sons to be faithful to God's will and to hope in God's ability to raise them from the dead. Mary's heart, pierced even deeper, fulfills even more perfectly this mother's love, courage, and fidelity.[45]

The mother of the Maccabees always retained her awe of God's miraculous formation of seven little bodies in her own body. Though these seven bodies later became her seven sorrows, her permanent wonder allowed her to see past the body parts lying on the ground that had swallowed up the blood of her beloved sons. Instead, she saw the beauty and splendor of God's goodness in creation. That vision sustained her through her loss of everything.

The mother of the Messiah, Our Lady of Seven Sorrows, had that vision, too. When Jesus looked down from the Cross and saw her beautiful, serene face, silently accepting his death as the sacrifice he offered for us, he immediately made her own sacrifice fruitful: *"Woman, behold, your son!"* (John 19:26). He gave his own mother to the new people of God, the Church. Next to the salvation he gained for the world, is there any more perfect gift he could have given to us?

— *Pondering the Mother of Martyrs* —

The mother of the Maccabees suffered because she had to
endure watching all her children suffer and die. Whether
or not we are parents, all of us have likely experienced the
suffering that comes to us as we watch the suffering of others.
We can clearly see that the suffering of the mother and her
sons was a test of their faith. Should they give up on God?
Were they tempted to charge him with neglect or, even
worse, impotence, because he allowed them to undergo such
merciless pain?

- Is your faith being tested in this way now? Can you start
  where the mother started when she had to suffer her
  extraordinary agony? She began with remembering
  that the miracle of human existence comes by God's
  own loving design and will. If he is the cause of our
  lives in this world, can you trust him to wisely see you
  and all of us through to its end?

The mother urged her last son to look beyond the horror
around him and see, instead, creation, with its evident beauty,
order, and wonder. The Scriptures often encourage us to do
the same. "*For from the greatness and beauty of created things
comes a corresponding perception of their Creator*" (Wisdom
13:5). St. Paul echoed this in his epistle to the Romans: "*Ever
since the creation of the world his* [that is, God's] *invisible nature,
namely, his eternal power and deity, has been clearly perceived in
the things that have been made*" (Romans 1:20).

- Do you need this encouragement from the world around us today?

The brothers were confident that God would bring good from the suffering that had befallen them. Is it too much of a stretch for you to believe that, too? St. Augustine can be of help here: "For almighty God ... because he is supremely good, would never allow any evil whatsoever to exist in his works if he were not so all-powerful and good as to cause good to emerge from evil itself" (CCC 311). Jesus invited us to share in his suffering by taking up our own crosses as we follow him (see Matthew 16:24–25). When we join our suffering to his, it becomes part of his redemptive suffering that saved the whole world (see Colossians 1:24).

- This truth does not minimize or eliminate our suffering, but it tells us that it is not *meaningless*. Does that help?

For those of us who are raising children, the mother of the Maccabees can be a helpful example of godly parenting. Perhaps Mary, too, was encouraged by her story as she and Joseph raised their unique son. The seven sons all grew up with a mother whose life shows evidence of these characteristics:

She never forgot God's miracle of conception in her womb; it convinced her that with God, nothing is impossible.

She always counted on God's goodness, a goodness to which the whole universe bears testimony. Even her experience of painful tragedy did not cause her to doubt it.

She raised her sons to know God's laws, to understand the covenant they, as Jews, were sealed into with him. They knew the Scripture stories (i.e., Moses) that revealed the history of God's unfailing mercy to his people. She believed her family's fidelity to this covenant was the ultimate purpose of all their lives.

She was confident there was nothing to fear in life, not even death, because human lives are always and continuously in God's wise hands.

- The mother of the martyrs in Maccabees communicated all this to her sons by word and example. Can this be helpful to you as you raise your children?

For some of us, the most dramatic moment in this story comes when the mother, after watching six of her sons butchered, leaned close to the seventh son and urged him to look beyond his brothers' blood and bones "*at heaven and earth*" and recognize God's great power in creating them out of nothing. She did not want the terrifying vision of what he could see all around them to blind him to the vision of what truly mattered. St. Paul gives us this same explicit counsel:

> *If then you have been raised with Christ, seek the things that are above, where Christ is, seated at the right hand of God. Set your minds on things that are above, not on things that are on earth. For you have died, and your life is hidden with Christ in God. When Christ who is your life appears, then you also will appear with him in glory.* (Colossians 3:1–4)

- Can this help you set your own gaze on what truly matters today?

Are there any lingering impressions from the mother of the Maccabees' life that you do not want to forget? Perhaps you can write them down here or in your own journal.

....

....

....

....

....

....

....

....

....

....

....

....

Chapter Twelve

Mary—In the Time of Messianic Fulfillment and the Church

"Who is this that looks forth like the dawn, fair as the moon,
bright as the sun, terrible as an army with banners?"

–Song of Solomon 6:10

Historical Context: Messianic Fulfillment (AD 1–AD 33)

"For behold, the winter is past, the rain is over and gone. The flowers appear on the earth, the time of pruning has come, and the voice of the turtledove is heard in our land... Arise, my love, my fair one, and come away" (Song of Solomon 2:11–13).
On a wall in my study, in addition to Rembrandt's painting of the holy woman Anna, with which we began our journey into the Old Testament, is a print of another famous work of art. It is Botticelli's *Madonna of the Book*. Although the two are different in nearly every way—in subjects, form, lines, use of light, and so on—they share a common theme. In the Rembrandt piece, we saw the old woman, Anna, lost in contemplation of the large book before her, with her hand lovingly caressing its words. We know

that in her devout, ascetical life she spent all the years of her widowhood worshipping God in the Jerusalem Temple. She was there at the very moment Simeon pronounced blessing on God for the child, Jesus, as well as words of prophecy to his mother. Hearing those words, she recognized and instantly proclaimed the child as the beginning of Israel's redemption to all who were there. Anna knew that the words she had read over and over in her long life were ultimately about these two people, mother and child, and their mission. From its very first pages, God promised the appearance of a mother and her son who would defeat the Enemy and undo the havoc the Devil wreaked on creation. For Anna, the Scriptures were brought to life that day in the appearance of Mary and Jesus in the Temple. Much later in this story, two disciples of Jesus met him after his Resurrection as a stranger on the road to Emmaus (see Luke 24:13–35). They also experienced how the full meaning of the Old Testament, even to people devoted to it as they were, was not revealed until the Incarnation. As they walked together with Jesus, he opened the *meaning* of the Scriptures to them, setting their hearts on fire and enabling them to recognize him in the breaking of bread.

In Botticelli's *Madonna of the Book*, the young, beautiful Mary is also focused on a book. The book is not named in the painting's title, but it is often described as "the book of hours," a devotional text popular in medieval times. It contained passages of Scripture, prayers, and hymns, as well as glorious artwork. Instead, I like to think of the book upon which Mary gazes as the Old Testament Scriptures, the same words Anna loved. Mary, like Anna, would have known its stories from childhood. Jesus is on her lap, but he is looking up at Mary, not at the book. Mary's right hand is lovingly placed on one its pages, with Jesus' infant hand on top of hers. Her other hand wraps around the baby, with one finger pointing to the book. Again, we see Jesus' hand on hers. Mary seems to have both the baby and the book in her field of vision. There, too, in her field of vision, is a bracelet of a crown of thorns on the child's arm, as well as a tiny scepter in his hand. The painting gloriously depicts how these two people, Jesus and Mary, are the culmination of the Old Covenant Scriptures. All the history, all the stories of men and women who walked with God, all the words of the prophets, all the beauty and wisdom of the poetry in its pages point forward to these two people. The painting's rich colors and textures in their bodies and clothing, the flowers blooming in the bowl beside them, even the first light of dawn seen in the window behind them all bring to life the promises of that beloved book on the table.

Yet there is something more to see here. As Mary looks down on the Scriptures and the child, Jesus looks up at her. There is tender, loving communion between them in this moment. This exquisitely expresses the supernatural power of the Scriptures, both the Old Testament and New Testament. Reading Scripture is not simply an educational exercise. It is, above all else, a communion with the Word of God himself, Jesus. In his Word, we see him, and he sees us. That explains why both Anna and Mary, in their separate paintings, are laying their hands on the book. They hungered for that communion. We should, too. As St. Paul wrote in his letter to the Romans, *"For whatever was written in former days was written for our instruction, that by steadfastness and by the encouragement of the Scriptures we might have hope"* (Romans 15:4). How might this great truth have worked in Mary's life? We have already considered many possible answers to that question in each chapter of this book. Now, we want to look for evidence of *when* Mary might have spent time pondering the Scriptures in her heart. Certainly, there were many such times; we will reflect on some of them.

Mary "considered in her mind what sort of greeting this might be" (Luke 1:29)

In Mary's story, when do we first see evidence that she was a woman who took into her mind and heart—pondered—the mysterious events that unfolded in her life? It appears at the Annunciation, when we first meet her. The angel, Gabriel, greeted her with extraordinary words: *"Hail, full of grace, the Lord is with you!"* In response, Mary *"was greatly troubled at the saying, and considered in her mind what sort of greeting this might be"* (Luke 1:28–29).

Before we know anything else about Mary, we see a trait in her that has come to characterize her from that day to this. At the time of the Annunciation, she was already a thoughtful, prayerful, contemplative woman. She considered *"in her mind"* what Gabriel's greeting might mean. In other words, Mary pondered what was happening to her. She would have understood that Gabriel appeared to her on God's behalf; perhaps she wondered why he addressed her as *"full of grace"* and not by her name.

We know that in St. Luke's Gospel the phrase *"full of grace"* interprets the Greek word *kecharitomene*. It meant that Mary was already filled with divine life. For Gabriel to use this word to address her rather than addressing her by name gave it the quality of a title that was already conferred on her before his appearance in Nazareth. Was it an understanding of this significance that *"greatly troubled"* Mary? She knew the only woman who had ever been filled with divine life was Eve, when God created her from Adam's side. Mary must have felt a shock when Gabriel addressed her as he did. Apparently, she had never thought of herself in such terms. So, she took the words of Gabriel's greeting into her mind, to "consider" them, to find their meaning.

If she spent a few moments remembering Eve's story, what might have come to mind about her? Eve shared God's own breath that he breathed into Adam, from whose flesh and bone she came. She was Adam's helper in the fruitful dominion God gave them over his creation. She was the *"mother of all living"* (Genesis 3:20). Unforgettably, Eve was also the central player in the great drama that unfolded in Eden, when the Serpent presented her with a choice that would affect all creation. Mary would also have remembered the promise God made when Eve chose badly. God told his enemy, the Serpent, to be on the alert for another man and woman, a mother and her son, who would fight their battle against him to the end and win. Because both Adam and Eve had been in a state of grace, undoubtedly the mother and son promised by God would, too.

As Mary quietly pondered Gabriel's greeting, he spoke again to her. *"Do not be afraid, Mary, for you have found favor with God"* (Luke 1:30). Gabriel sought to comfort her by assuring her that God intended to bless her in this visit. In the words of Fr. Garrigou-Lagrange, "Joy and confidence succeeded reverential fear and astonishment as the angel spoke."[46]

To direct Mary's heart and mind toward the blessing God intended for her, Gabriel began to reveal the reason for his visit. We know, because of the Church's long history of pondering Mary as the New Eve, that she was preserved, by an act of God's grace, from the stain of original sin. As the *Catechism* teaches, she is "redeemed, in a more exalted fashion, by reason of the merits of her Son" and "by the grace of God" she "remained free of every personal sin her whole life long" (CCC 492–493). This should not surprise us. Mary and the son she bore were, from Eden, promised to be always and victoriously on God's side in the great battle between his goodness and his enemy's evil. God himself prepared them both for this *"before the foundation of the world,"* a blessing that will someday extend to us as well (see Ephesians 1:4).

Gabriel explained to Mary that she would give birth to a son to be named Jesus. God would give him the throne of David, and he would rule over a kingdom that would last forever. Mary asked, *"How can this be, since I have no husband?"* (Luke 1:34). She was curious about how she could conceive a child, not doubtful that she would. Mary's question suggests that although she was soon to be married to Joseph, himself a descendant of David, she had no expectation of becoming a mother, for reasons not explained in Scripture.

In answer to her question, Gabriel explained that God would cause her son to be conceived in her without the agency of a man, making the child *"holy, the Son of God"* (see Luke 1:35). The word he used to describe this action of God, *"overshadow,"* is also used in the Greek version of Exodus 40:35, when God overshadowed or *"filled"* the Tabernacle Moses built in the wilderness, making it God's dwelling place as the Israelites journeyed home to the Promised Land. So, Mary understood this would be no ordinary conception of a child! It would take a miracle. Gabriel went on to tell her that her elderly and formerly barren cousin, Elizabeth, had also conceived a child miraculously. He then used words that could have put Mary in mind of another such birth: *"For with God nothing will be impossible"* (Luke 1:37). This was essentially the same reminder an angelic messenger gave to Sarah, Abraham's barren wife: *"Is anything too hard for the LORD?"* (Genesis 18:14).

"Consider the ancient generations and see: who ever trusted in the Lord and was put to shame? Or who ever persevered in his commandments and was forsaken? Or who ever called upon him and was overlooked?" (Sirach 2:10)

We can see that from start to finish, Gabriel addressed Mary in language and events drawn from Sacred Scriptures. His greeting, *"Hail, full of grace,"* evoked the one woman in human history who had ever been full of divine life, Eve, and all that her story brings to life. He announced that Mary would give birth to a son of David who would rule over a kingdom without end. His words made sense because she knew about the covenant God made with David, as well as the Messianic expectation of God's people that someday his heir would appear to begin that reign again. Mary would have known, from Queen Bathsheba's life, that if she was this promised son's mother, she would be queen of that kingdom, the *gebirah* of Israel, reigning with her son. When Gabriel explained the "how" of this miraculous conception, he used the word *"overshadow,"* a liturgical word familiar to Jews. It described God's descent on the wilderness Tabernacle, when he filled it with his holy presence. To speak that way must have helped Mary understand God's union with her in her body guaranteed her son's holiness, as well as her own. Finally, to encourage her to receive the plan that was laid out before her, Gabriel used another angel's words to remind her of Sarah and how God had made laughter for her, because nothing is too hard for God.

The Annunciation is remarkable in more ways than we can count, but we should be sure to include in that number the overwhelming evidence that Mary's mind and heart were full of God's revelation in the Old Testament. Why would Gabriel have addressed her in the way he did—grounded so deeply in its words and their meanings—if she had not been able to understand and receive his message?

"Behold, I am the handmaid of the Lord; let it be to me according to your word" (Luke 1:38)

Let us pause here to allow ourselves time to absorb this moment in salvation history. The words are very familiar to us, but the thrill of hearing them should be new each time they reach our ears. To help us in this is a reflection from a homily by St. Bernard of Clairvaux:

> Virgin, you have heard ... that you will conceive and bear a son; you have heard that it will be by the Holy Spirit and not by a man. The angel is waiting for your reply ... We, too, are waiting for this merciful word, my lady, we who are miserably weighed down under a sentence of condemnation. The price of our salvation is being offered you. If you consent, we shall immediately be set free. We all have been made in the eternal Word of God, and look, we are dying. In your brief reply we shall be restored and so brought back to life ... [T]he whole world is waiting, bowed down at your feet. And rightly so, because on your answer depends the comfort of the afflicted, the redemption of captives, the deliverance of the damned; the salvation of all the sons of Adam, your whole race ... Behold, the long-desired of all nations is standing at the door and knocking ... Get up, run, open! Get up by faith, run by prayer, open by consent! ... 'Behold', she said, 'I am the handmaiden of the Lord.'[47]

The greatness of Mary's *fiat* (meaning "let it be done") has inspired volumes of art, poetry, meditations, theology, and prayers for centuries. Why? It is because God began his healing of creation with Mary's cooperation. When Eve heeded the words of a fallen angel, she grasped at death for herself and all of us. She cooperated with the Enemy in his rebellion against God. When Mary heeded the words of an angel sent from God, the pure heart of this simple girl in Nazareth opened completely to receive God's plan for her and the whole world. She cooperated with God in his plan for its redemption. Is it any wonder that her loving obedience has inspired countless souls from that day to this to follow her example?

Both Mary and Eve were capable of freely choosing to return God's love for them by obedience to his will, but while Eve chose badly, Mary chose well. What was the difference between these two women? Eve lived in the pristine beauty of the Garden of Eden, unblemished by the shadow of sin. Mary lived in a small village, in the world that was blighted ever since that shadow first fell on it. But God preserved Mary from the stain of original sin, through the merits of the son she would bear. His gracious act spared her, as well, from its mark, the inclination to sin left in all of us born into it. He prepared her this way to help solve man's only problem, sin.

Mary was filled with grace, showered with blessings by the One who chose her from eternity to be his mother, the Mother of God. One of these blessings, Fr. Garrigou-Lagrange tells us, is that Mary "had by a special privilege a knowledge of the Scriptures greater than that of any of the saints."[48] This was a great gift to Mary. From the Sacred Scriptures, she was well acquainted with countless faithful men and women who obeyed God, no matter the cost. Mary's life was permeated by vivid examples of women who loved and obeyed God, many of whom we have come to know in this book. From them, she learned the trustworthiness of God, his faithfulness to his promises, and the rich fruitfulness of doing his will. Did her formation in the Old Testament fortify her to receive God's will in humility? Although Gabriel addressed her as one full of divine life, in her response to him she spoke in the way she had always thought of herself: "the *handmaid of the Lord.*" Was she thinking about Hannah and Bathsheba, who also identified themselves that way? Was she remembering Rahab, who risked everything to help God save his people, saying, "*According to your words, so be it*" (Joshua 2:21)? In humility, faith, and with great courage, Mary said yes to God. With her yes, she brought into the world the Messiah, Christ the Lord, who is "yes" to all God's promises to us. As St. Paul wrote, *all the promises of God find their Yes in him*" (2 Corinthians 1:20).

"In those days Mary arose and went with haste into the hill country ... and greeted Elizabeth" (Luke 1:39–40)

After "*the angel departed from her*" (Luke 1:38), Mary hurried to visit Elizabeth in "*the hill country.*" From Nazareth, this was a trip of some distance, between eighty and one hundred miles. It is very likely Mary walked, for only wealthy people could afford better transportation. She was possibly accompanied by someone, because she had to travel through high hills where danger from robbers always lurked. To reach Elizabeth's home would take four or five days. Mary had lots of time to think.

We know that Mary was a human person; she was not divine in any way, though she was given many extraordinary gifts by God. She was not hobbled by sin like us, but she was not omniscient, not all-knowing. As we follow her on this journey to visit Elizabeth, we can imagine she had to absorb what happened at the Annunciation. She needed to think over what Gabriel revealed about God's plan for her, as well as what he did not reveal. This kind of pondering would have come naturally to her, as we have already noted. What might have been on her mind as she walked those dusty miles?

In his visit to Mary, Gabriel spoke primarily about the son to be born to her. His few words were spent on describing his greatness, his holiness, his meaning for God's people, all taken from Scripture. When he answered Mary's question about how she would conceive a child, the details he gave her were brief, focused more on the consequences of the "how"—the son would be called *"holy, the Son of God"* (Luke 1:35)—than on her experience of it. Perhaps Mary, too, on her trip to visit Elizabeth spent her hours thinking about her son as Israel's Messiah. She knew enough from the Sacred Scriptures to contemplate what his appearance would bring about. In her day, there was heightened expectation and hope for the long-awaited Messiah's arrival. A king of David's house to sit again on Israel's throne meant liberation and joy, the exuberant delight of people who experienced God's faithfulness to his promises. The Jews could live the way King David had once asked of God: *"Keep me as the apple of the eye; hide me in the shadow of your wings"* (Psalm 17:8). While popular expectation looked to the Messiah to restore national prestige, Mary surely knew that he would enable Israel to know how much God loved them.

At the Annunciation, in humility, she freely received God's plan for herself and, as the New Eve, for us and all creation as well. She said little. In the words of Fr. Garrigou-Lagrange, "Though her joy at the birth of her Son was intense, she treasured it up in silence ... God's greatest actions defy human expression. What could Mary say to equal what she had experienced?"[49] When she reached Elizabeth's home, though, she would speak, and her words would resound to all generations to come.

"My soul magnifies the Lord, and my spirit rejoices in God my Savior" (Luke 1:47)

We can imagine Mary arriving at Elizabeth's home full of all her pondering on the road. Perhaps she was wondering where to begin her conversation with her cousin. She called out a greeting to Elizabeth. She suddenly discovered she did not need to plan her words. This simple greeting had a profound result, almost as unexpected and glorious as the effect Gabriel's greeting in Nazareth had on Mary (see Luke 1:38–45). Elizabeth's baby, John the Baptist, *"leaped in her womb"* at the sound of Mary's voice. At this, Elizabeth was *"filled with the Holy Spirit."* Gabriel had spoken of *"the Holy Spirit"* who would *"overshadow"* Mary. If Elizabeth was *"filled with the Holy Spirit,"* we should pay close attention to what she said to Mary.

With *"a loud cry,"* Elizabeth exclaimed, *"Blessed are you among women, and blessed is the fruit of your womb!"* The first words out of Elizabeth's mouth were blessings on Mary and her child. The blessing on Mary is not new to us. Twice before in Scripture these words were pronounced over women—on Jael (Judges 5:24) and on Judith (Judith 13:18). In salvation history, those two holy women destroyed the head of an enemy of God's people. Here, Elizabeth, *"filled with the Holy Spirit,"* hearkened back to them to bless Mary. Immediately we are taken back to Eden and the promise God made to send a mother-warrior and her victor-son into battle against his enemy, delivering a death blow to his head. If ever we need biblical evidence that both Mary and Jesus would work together to fulfill God's plan for our salvation, we find it right here.

Elizabeth explained the impact just the sound of Mary's voice had on John the Baptist—*"joy!"* She also marveled over the gift of a visit from mother and son. *"Why is this granted me, that the mother of my Lord should come to me?"* Elizabeth and John in her womb recognized, by the Holy Spirit's fullness in them, that in the appearance of young, pregnant Mary of Nazareth, they were honored to have both the new King of Israel and his queen mother under their roof. No wonder they both erupted in joy.

Elizabeth's Spirit-filled blessing on Mary continued: *"And blessed is she who believed that there would be a fulfillment of what was spoken to her from the Lord."* The first part of Elizabeth's blessing expanded Mary's understanding of what lay ahead for her and her son, the Messiah—together they would battle God's enemy. The second part of her blessing was solely in response to Mary's faith. Indeed, it was Mary's faith that enabled her *fiat.* Elizabeth was the first person in salvation history to express all of humanity's gratitude to Mary, the New Eve, who chose to believe God rather than his enemy.

Here, at last, we will see what was in Mary's mind and heart, because, in response to Elizabeth's words, she did not keep her thoughts inside. She was bursting with joy and gladness, for herself and for God's majestic love, mercy, and care for his people. Perhaps she was thinking about Miriam, the first woman to sing aloud God's praises for victory over an enemy. It is likely that she was thinking about Hannah, who sang of God's power and mercy granted in the miraculous birth of a son. She could have been remembering Deborah and Judith, women of courage and faith, who likewise knew that songs of praise were fitting when God overturned an enemy by the hands of his lowly handmaidens. It is not an unreasonable stretch to see the stories of Old Testament women filling Mary's mind and heart in this moment.

Mary's beloved canticle, the *Magnificat*, sprang from her lips (see Luke 1:46–55). She, like so many women of faith who lived before her, could not contain her joy anymore. Her song, that has never been forgotten by *"all generations"* coming after her, overflows with delight and gratitude that the Almighty had done *"great things"* for her and *"holy is his name."* In words chosen almost entirely from the Old Testament that she loved, Mary extolled God's desire to turn the tables on the proud and arrogant, upending appearances throughout human history. She recounted how God lifted the humble, fed the hungry, liberated the oppressed, had mercy on the faithful. Mary's canticle, whenever it is sung, cleanses the earth from the stench of that vicious lie that found its way into Eve's mind and heart. God is on our side, because he is our Father; we can trust him.

"Behold, this child is set ... for a sign that is spoken against (and a sword will pierce through your own soul also)" (Luke 2:34–35)

We have been looking for evidence of when Mary might have found understanding and encouragement in pondering stories of Old Testament women. The Annunciation was one such occasion; the trip from Nazareth to the hill country of Elizabeth's home was another. Now, during the Presentation of Jesus in the Temple (see Luke 2:22–38), we find something new for Mary to receive. Gabriel's message and Elizabeth's greeting had filled her mind and heart with bright joy and gratitude, so evident in her *Magnificat*. But there was pain, too. In the words of Fr. Garrigou-Lagrange, "Mary said her *Fiat* in peace and holy joy on the day of the Annunciation. There was sorrow too in her heart at the thought of the sufferings which … [the prophet Isaiah] had foretold would befall her Son. Still more light is thrown for her on the mystery of the Redemption when the holy old man Simeon speaks."[50] Because Mary was a contemplative young woman, she surely spent time thinking prayerfully about what she heard in the Temple that day.

Mary and Joseph took the infant Jesus to the Temple to observe Jewish laws for parents after giving birth to a first son. Simeon, a Spirit-filled man who recognized the child as the promised Messiah, took the babe in his arms and blessed God and his parents. Then he prophesied to Mary. Speaking directly to her, he announced a future for mother and child that would include opposition and a piercing sword. From Elizabeth, Mary heard a Scriptural blessing that suggested victory over an enemy—a future battle—but Simeon went further. What lay ahead for mother and son was not a generalized battle between good and evil. No, this would be a personal battle. Mary's son would cause *"the fall and rising of many in Israel"* (Luke 2:34). He would stand at the center of great division. Jesus would be the dividing line between life and death, and for that he would be opposed, *"spoken against."* Swords would be drawn, and neither Mary nor her son would be spared their piercing pain.

From the time of Jesus' conception and especially at his birth—when angels sang in the sky and shepherds rejoiced at the manger—there had been glory and joy in God's plan. At the same time, Mary would have known the Old Testament prophecies of Isaiah that foretold the coming of a Suffering Servant. With Simeon's words, Mary could not avoid realizing what being the mother of this son would mean for both of them. *"And when they had performed everything according to the law of the Lord* [in Jerusalem]*, they returned ... to Nazareth"* (Luke 2:39). The distance between Jerusalem and Nazareth was about a hundred miles. It would have taken several days to walk, especially traveling with an infant. Once again, Mary was on a dusty road with plenty of time to think. As Fr. Garrigou-Lagrange writes, "Joy and sorrow are wedded in the heart of the Mother of God ... Her faith in the mystery of the Redemption expands."[51]

When she thought about the trouble that lay ahead for her as mother of the Messiah, did Mary think of other faithful Old Testament mothers whose lives were marked by this unique kind of suffering? She might have thought of Eve, who lived through the death of one son and the permanent departure of the other yet was still able to see God's personal care for her and rejoice at the birth of Seth. Perhaps she remembered the desperate widow whose fear of losing her two sons to slavery drove her to seek help from the holy man, Elisha, who answered her need in a superabundance of riches. Surely the brave mother of the Maccabees came to her mind, whose seven sons died nobly for their obedience to God. Even though this mother lost her own life, she never wavered in her confidence that death was not the end for her and her sons. If Mary went over and over these details, we can imagine that they fueled the hope in her heart. As Fr. Garrigou-Lagrange leads us to meditate, Mary's hope "was a perfect confidence and trust which relied not on self but on the divine mercy and omnipotence. It was therefore sure."[52] Certainly, she gave herself in peace to her mother's vocation in

Nazareth. *"And the child grew and became strong, filled with wisdom; and the favor of God was upon him"* (Luke 2:40).

"Son, why have you treated us so? ... your father and I have been looking for you anxiously" (Luke 2:48)

Twelve years have passed since we last heard Mary speak in Elizabeth's home. Her words then brimmed with joy. When Jesus was twelve years old, he went with his family on pilgrimage to Jerusalem for Passover (see Luke 2:41-52). When the feast ended, Mary, Joseph, and their entourage of family and friends left for home. Jesus stayed behind without telling them. Upon discovering he was missing, his parents spent three anguished days searching the city for him. They found him in the Temple, amazing all who heard him with *"his understanding and his answers."*

His parents, too, were *"astonished,"* not because of what he was saying, but because of what he did to them. We hear Mary speak again, and this time her words are full of pain. The question she put to Jesus was the question of the ages, the question all humanity has thought and asked ever since our first parents were expelled from the Garden. It was expressed poetically centuries earlier in the book of Job, the ancient story of a righteous man confounded by what God had allowed to happen to him: *"Why have you made me your mark? Why have I become a burden to you?"* (Job 7:20). The Psalmist, too, anguished over God's seeming indifference to his suffering: *"My God, my God, why have you forsaken me?"* (Psalm 22:1). Jesus, when he was dying on the Cross, would ask this profoundly human question, taking up the Psalmist's cry (see Matthew 27:46). When we experience suffering or see the suffering all around us in this world, do not all of us want to ask

God, *"Why have you treated us so?"* For Mary to ask this of Jesus makes us recognize our need to pause and carefully consider it.

What did Mary do after expressing the pain of these words? Fr. Garrigou-Lagrange tells us, "Mary accepted in faith what she could not as yet understand. The depth and the extent of the Mystery of the Redemption will be revealed to her only gradually. She is glad to have found Jesus again. But in her joy sounds many an overtone of sadnesses yet to come."[53] Jesus would save us from sin by dying for us on the Cross, giving us the opportunity to offer our pain up to him, giving it meaning. And Mary would be united to her son in that sacrifice.

Once again, we find Mary walking on the road from Jerusalem to Nazareth. We know that when Jesus answered her question in the Temple, his parents *"did not understand the saying which he spoke to them"* (Luke 2:50). On the journey home of several days, Mary had time to take into her mind and heart all that had happened. As Jeanne Kun has written,

> Though Mary does not grasp what Jesus means by his answer, she offers no further objection to the anxiety he had caused them. Her response is not a closed, offended silence, but an attentive stillness as she turns over in her mind the mystery of her son's identity and his strange words.[54]

As Mary walked mile after mile on quiet, country roads, did she think of Hannah, the woman who, at the Temple in Shiloh, offered back to God her only son, the one for whom she longed and prayed so many years? Perhaps she recalled Hannah's fruitfulness after she let Samuel go, birthing five more children. It must have been clear to Mary that even at the age of twelve—

the beginning of manhood in Jewish life—Jesus knew that service to his Father in heaven came before all else in his life. She knew that his presence in the Temple rather than with his parents was only the *appearance* of failed love. Jesus' answer to Mary could be phrased this way: "The only reason I am here is to do my Father's work. It is not from a lack of love for you; it could never be that. You must trust me, no matter how it looks." Then he proved his love by going home with his parents and being obedient to them.

"And he went down with them ... to Nazareth, and was obedient to them; and his mother kept all these things in her heart" (Luke 2:51)

When the Holy Family resumed life in Nazareth, they entered a long stretch of time the Church calls "the hidden years" (CCC 531–534). Scripture is completely silent on them, a silence finally broken when Jesus began his public ministry at age thirty. These eighteen years provide us with our final opportunity to consider how the rich testimony from holy women who lived before Mary may have been part of her preparation to fulfill her mission as mother of the Messiah.

We recognized in the episode of Jesus in the Temple the first hint of a coming change in his relationship with his mother. Surprisingly, it was Mary rather than Joseph, the head of the family, who put the question of his painful disappearance to him. Already, the uniqueness of their relationship was highlighted. Presumably, during the hidden years, this would intensify. As St. John Paul II has written,

> although his mother introduced Jesus to the culture and traditions of the people of Israel, from the time of his finding

in the Temple, he would reveal his full awareness of being the Son of God, sent to spread the truth in the world and exclusively follow the Father's will. From being her Son's 'teacher,' Mary thus became the humble disciple of the divine Master to whom she had given birth.[55]

In the Temple, Jesus and the teachers were reading and discussing Sacred Scripture, a common practice there and in all synagogues. In his public ministry, from beginning to end, he consciously lived his life as a fulfillment of Scripture. He quoted its verses, referred to its history, and compared himself to its heroes. We can assume that as Jesus gradually became Mary's teacher in their hidden years, discussion of Scripture, especially of its heroic women, was an essential part of the lessons he shared with her.

Let us consider one example of how Mary's years of formation by Jesus—accomplished away from the eyes of the world—prepared her for the work she was born to do. Recall her pain in losing sight of Jesus for three days in Jerusalem when he was twelve. Much later, as Jesus began his public ministry, it was Mary who requested him to perform his first miracle at Cana, an act that would be their first foray into the battle they must lead. Mary knew the miracle would hasten Jesus' *"hour,"* when she and her son would feel the piercing pain of a sword. Upon finding Jesus in the Temple, Mary was hurt by his separation from her. In Cana, she stepped into her heroic moment and willingly accepted it. In the hidden years with Jesus, did he teach Mary to meditate on the stories of heroic, courageous Old Testament women—Rahab, Deborah, Jael, Esther, Judith, the mother of the Maccabees—as he opened her eyes to see herself in all of them?

Mary, of course, remained his mother. From infancy to adulthood, her role was to help her son mature in human wisdom (see Luke 2:52) to prepare for his mission. Within the context of their ordinary lives in Nazareth, the boy who, at the age of twelve, astonished all those in the Temple with his remarkable knowledge and understanding gradually became the man who helped his mother enter her vocation as his helper in the work of redemption. She was not only his mother, but, as the New Eve, she was the mother of *"the rest of her offspring ... those who keep the commandments of God and bear testimony to Jesus"* (Revelation 12:17).

As we pondered the lives of so many Old Testament types of Mary, we easily imagined how their stories could have been part of her formation as mother of the Messiah. The Old Testament women did not, themselves, know what their stories would one day mean. They simply lived in humility and faith in obedience to their Lord. It was God's hand that wove their stories into the great tapestry of his plan for creation. The tapestry, of course, is not finished. We, too, are being woven into it. What will our part of the story tell? We can now turn to Mary for help answering this question.

"Behold, your mother!" (John 19:27)

Jesus, dying on the Cross, exhorted the one disciple who had not deserted him to receive his mother as his own. He did not say, "Take care of this woman as you would your own mother." His words directed John to *"behold"* Mary, to see, to observe her, to set his vision upon her. Mary was full of grace, full of divine life. For John to look upon Mary meant that although Jesus would be separated from his friends for three days, they could be comforted by seeing Mary's face that looked so much like his. They could watch her live through this painful time as one whose perfect faith, hope, and love kept her steady, without fear. She could be their teacher until they were ready to teach the whole world about Jesus.

Countless words about Mary's example as a follower of Jesus have been written through the ages. We have space to consider only a few.

"I am the handmaid of the Lord" (Luke 1:38)

Gabriel addressed Mary as a woman highly favored by God. However, Mary identified herself as *"the handmaid of the Lord,"* his servant. She teaches us the foundational virtue for women of grace—humility. We are always to live in smallness before God, as well as before others. Mary's humility was the antidote to Eve's pride in Eden. Jesus called us to this humility, as well: *"The Son of man came not to be served but to serve"* (Matthew 20:28). How might our days be different if we began each of them by looking in a mirror and saying to ourselves, "Good morning, handmaid of the Lord"?

"Let it be to me according to your word" (Luke 1:38)

Mary loved the Word of God—written in the Sacred Scriptures, announced by an angel, alive in her womb. Her mind and heart, even her body, were full of God's Word. Because of what Jesus accomplished for us, we can likewise be devoted to the Word of God in all the ways he comes to us. He is there when we read the Bible, both the Old Testament and New Testament. We can commit ourselves to be as fluent in Scripture as Mary was, receiving its nourishment so vital to our souls. We receive the Word of God, Jesus, in the sacramental life of the Church, preeminently in the Eucharist, the Bread of Heaven. Can we put this prayer in our minds and hearts each day: "Father, your Word is a lamp to my feet and a light on my path. May it be to me according to your Word"?

"My soul proclaims the greatness of the Lord" (Luke 1:46)

In her prayer song, the *Magnificat*, Mary followed the tradition of her mothers in faith by proclaiming—magnifying—the greatness of God. All these women teach us a crucial lesson about the life of grace. Our minds and hearts should overflow with praise and gratitude for the goodness, mercy, and power of God. Our prayers should always begin there, rejecting the Serpent's lie in Eden about God's character. If we start our prayers with ourselves, we lose our way. Our needs and our problems can dwarf God in our minds. Can we avoid this by starting our prayers with Mary's words: "Father, you have done great things for me, and holy is your name"?

"Mary kept all these things, pondering them in her heart" (Luke 2:19)

Mary was a woman who took into her mind and heart the events of her life as they unfolded. She did this before she spoke. We cannot miss this defining quality of her life—she moved through it in simplicity, stillness, silence. This gave her both time and opportunity to ponder. Mary's pondering was not primarily a mental activity. It was not a matter of just thinking things through. She began with thoughts, as we all do, but she took her thoughts into her heart. She put all her first reactions, questions, and confusions into the filter of love. This is a profound lesson for us. We live in a loud, talkative, opinionated culture. Our reactions can easily slip into words that are shared everywhere, with everyone. Has there ever been an age as verbose and lacking in propriety as ours? To ponder as Mary did, in both mind and heart, takes practice. If we take the time to follow her example, we will see the immediate improvement it makes in everyday living.

"Do whatever he tells you" (John 2:5)

Mary lived these words before she spoke them to the servants at the Cana wedding and to us. As the Vatican II document *Lumen Gentium* reminds us, "she devoted herself totally as a handmaid of the Lord to the person and work of her Son, under Him and with Him, by the grace of almighty God, serving the mystery of redemption."[56] Her words exhort us to be obedient servants of Jesus, yet the example of her life shows that our obedience to him is not simply servile. No, our obedience is a privilege, a grace that allows us to participate in the "mystery of redemption" in the world. To do whatever Jesus tells us is not a loss of freedom. Rather, it is a bold step into the liberating freedom from anything in us that threatens to sabotage the life of grace he wants to give us. Mary, in her maternal wisdom, calls us to follow Jesus as she did. Mary was the perfection of all that inspired us in the Old Testament women we have met in this book. Those women taught Mary, and Mary teaches us. Let us ask Mother Mary to pray we have her courage to do whatever her son tells us today.

Endnotes

1. Scott Hahn, ed., *Catholic Bible Dictionary* (New York: Doubleday Religion, 2008), 929.

2. Benedict XVI, *Verbum Domini* (September 30, 2019), 28.

3. Second Vatican Council, *Dei Verbum* (November 18, 1965), 25.

4. *Dei Verbum*, 12.

5. *Dei Verbum*, 25.

6. *Dei Verbum,* 25.

7. See Gertrud von le Fort, *The Eternal Woman: The Timeless Meaning of the Feminine,* trans. Marie Cecilia Buehrle (San Francisco: Ignatius, 2010), and St. John Paul II's Theology of the Body.

8. John Paul II, *Letter to Women* (June 29, 1995), 7.

9. John Paul II, *Theotokos: Woman, Mother, Disciple; A Catechesis on Mary, Mother of God* (Boston: Pauline Books and Media, 2000), 92.

10. Andrew of Crete, *Sermon 1 on the Dormition of Mary,* quoted in John Paul II, 92.

11. Taken from Suzanne Noffke, OP, ed. and trans., *The Letters of Catherine of Siena,* vol. 1, (Tempe, AZ: Arizona Center for Medieval and Renaissance Studies, 2001), vol. 203.

12. "The Exsultet: The Proclamation of Easter," United States Conference of Catholic Bishops (website), accessed August 23, 2023, usccb.org.

13. Joseph Cardinal Ratzinger, *Behold the Pierced One* (San Francisco: Ignatius, 1986), 119.

14. Tim Gray and Jeff Cavins, *Walking with God* (West Chester, PA: Ascension, 2010), 73.

15. Damasus Winzen, OSB, *Pathways in Scripture: A Book-by-Book Guide to the Spiritual Riches of the Bible* (Cincinnati: St. Anthony Messenger Press, 1976), 57.

16. Ambrose, *Concerning Virgins* 1.3.12.

17. Sister Agnes Maria of St. John, OP, private correspondence, used by permission; emphasis added.

18. Gray and Cavins, *Walking with God*, 120.

19. Gray and Cavins, 119.

20. Gray and Cavins, 119.

21. Origen, *Tractates on the Books of Holy Scripture* 12, quoted in John Bergsma and Brant Pitre, *A Catholic Introduction to the Bible: Old Testament* (San Francisco: Ignatius, 2018), 313.

22. Cyril of Jerusalem, *Catechetical Lectures* 2.9, quoted in Bergsma and Pitre, 313.

23. John Paul II, *Theotokos*, 61–62.

24. John Paul II, *Redemptoris Mater* (March 25, 1987), 20.

25. Origen, *Homilies on Judges* 5.5, quoted in Bergsma and Pitre, *A Catholic Introduction to the Bible*, 335.

26. Reginald Garrigou-Lagrange, OP, *The Mother of the Saviour and Our Interior Life*, trans. Bernard Kelly (1948; repr., Rockford, IL: TAN, 1993), 157.

27. Albert the Great, *Mariale* 42, quoted in Garrigou-Lagrange, 162.

28. Ambrose, *Concerning Widows* 8.47, 50, quoted in Bergsma and Pitre, *A Catholic Introduction to the Bible*, 335–336.

29. Winzen, *Pathways in Scripture*, 132.

30. Sarah Christmyer, *Becoming Women of the Word: How to Answer God's Call with Purpose and Joy; A Spiritual Pilgrimage Through the Old Testament* (Notre Dame, IN: Ave Maria, 2019), 94.

31. Augustine, *The City of God* 17.4, quoted in Bergsma and Pitre, *A Catholic Introduction to the Bible*, 375.

32. Edward Sri, *Rethinking Mary in the New Testament* (San Francisco: Ignatius; Greenwood Village, CO: Augustine Institute, 2018), 79.

33. *The Ignatius Catholic Study Bible: The New Testament; Revised Standard*

Version, Second Catholic Edition (San Francisco: Ignatius, 2010), 170.

34. In *The Great Adventure Catholic Bible* (West Chester, PA: Ascension, 2018), p. 622, note for Esther 11:2.

35. Christmyer, *Becoming Women of the Word*, 108–109.

36. John Paul II, *Theotokos*, 74–75.

37. Friedrich Justus Knecht, *A Practical Commentary on Holy Scripture* (Rockford, IL: TAN, 2003), 356.

38. Athanasius, *Festal Letters* 8, quoted in Bergsma and Pitre, *A Catholic Introduction to the Bible*, 593.

39. *Little Counsels of Mother Agnes of Jesus, OCD* (Grand Rapids, MI: 1982), quoted in *Magnificat* 24, no. 11: 312.

40. Bergsma and Pitre, *A Catholic Introduction to the Bible*, 481–482.

41. *1 Clement* 55.3–4, quoted in Bergsma and Pitre, 483.

42. Knecht, *A Practical Commentary on Holy Scripture*, 320.

43. Gray and Cavins, *Walking with God*, 230–231.

44. Knecht, *A Practical Commentary on Holy Scripture*, 365.

45. Gray and Cavins, *Walking with God*, 232.

46. Garrigou-Lagrange, *The Mother of the Saviour*, 99.

47. Bernard of Clairvaux, *Four Homilies in Praise of the Virgin Mother*, in Bernard of Clairvaux and Amadeus of Lausanne, *Magnificat: Homilies in Praise of the Blessed Virgin Mary*, trans. Marie-Bernard Saïd and Grace Perigo (Kalamazoo, MI: Cistercian Publications, 1979), 4.8–9.

48. Garrigou-Lagrange, *The Mother of the Saviour*, 126.

49. Garrigou-Lagrange, 111.

50. Garrigou-Lagrange, 111.

51. Garrigou-Lagrange, 112, 124.

52. Garrigou-Lagrange, 130.

53. Garrigou-Lagrange, 113.

54. Jeanne Kun, *My Soul Magnifies the Lord: A Scriptural Journey with Mary* (Ijamsville, MD: Word Among Us Press, 2003), 115.

55. John Paul II, *Theotokos*, 154.

56. Second Vatican Council, *Lumen Gentium* (November 21, 1964), 56.